ACCIDENTAL
KILLING

A Survivor's Handbook

W0007372

All proceeds from this book go to The Hyacinth Fellowship,
a 501c3 nonprofit charity

Printed in partnership with Crown Publishing, Fort Thomas, KY

ACCIDENTAL KILLING

A Survivor's Handbook

MARYANN JACOBI GRAY & CHRIS YAW

*To every good person who has done a bad thing,
may you find hope and healing here.*

Table of Contents

Preface

Welcome to a club nobody wants to belong to.

If you are reading this, it's likely you or someone you care about has unintentionally killed or seriously injured a person. Maybe it was a car crash or a firearm accident. Maybe there was a moment of distraction at work or at home. Maybe you gave somebody COVID.

You may be like the hundreds of people who regularly write about their experiences on our blog. You may be absolutely devastated to have taken a life, even though you didn't mean to—and regardless of whether it was your fault. You may feel like your life is forever changed and that you will never be at peace with yourself. You may be grieving, guilty, ashamed, afraid, or angry. You may feel numb and distant from others. You may be having difficulty concentrating. You might be sleeping too much or too little or eating too much or too little, and you might have physical symptoms like an upset stomach, headaches, or back pain. And you might endure frequent flashbacks, images, or memories of the accident—the sights, sounds, even the smells.

If you're feeling any—or all—of these things, we get it.

We, too, have unintentionally killed.

And we know that even if you are surrounded by loving family and friends who want to support you, they don't know what it's like to unintentionally harm someone.

They don't know the horror of that moment of impact.

They don't know the ongoing anguish of those lingering, haunting images. They don't know how this unintentional harm has destroyed our sense of self as good, responsible people. They don't understand why, since we intended no harm, we see ourselves as bad and undeserving of solace.

They don't understand how we cannot simply call it an "accident" and move on. And they don't understand our hidden pain. While we are not the victims, we carry tremendous emotional burdens of guilt, shame, embarrassment, and isolation because both our souls and our society have little sympathy for those who have done what we have done.

Unintentional harm is one of the most harmful, pervasive, and least talked about traumas humans endure. With this book, we offer a guide for healing for people who have caused unintentional harm—and those who care about them. The content has been developed through many years of conversation with others who have caused unintentional harm—as well as from our own experience. Maryann accidentally killed a young boy who darted in front of her car; a friend and gardener died at Chris's home because of a faulty garage door. We have been where you are, and we want you to know that you're not alone. There is hope.

Maryann began this project after suffering alone for more than 25 years. She and Chris wrote this book, but Maryann died before its publication from complications after a medical procedure. "This book is part of her legacy. Her heart's desire was for people who have caused unintentional harm to find healing and wholeness.

Maryann Jacobi Gray (1954-2023)
Founder, Hyacinth Fellowship

Chris Yaw
Co-founder and president of Hyacinth Fellowship

Accidental Killing:

A Survivor's Handbook

Introduction

As people who have caused unintentional death or serious injury, most of us feel like no one else in our world understands us or our situation. This makes us reluctant to talk about unintentional harm. So, it becomes a secret: There's no one to talk to who has shared the same experience and can offer reassurance and guidance. There's no role model or rule book on how to cope. You're on your own.

You may feel like Lisa, one of the hundreds of people who post on the website or reach out to us through the Hyacinth Fellowship, a worldwide organization serving the needs of those who have unintentionally killed or seriously injured other people. Lisa wrote:

> *Hi all, my accident happened two days ago. I can't go into details because of legal reasons, but I was driving, lost control, and went down an embankment into a river. I escaped the wreck, but my friend drowned. It has been a very rough two days as police haven't really kept me updated on what's happened. I have a great support network of family and friends, but I just can't get out of my head that I shouldn't get to enjoy things if I've just robbed someone of that. I have no idea how his family are, which is killing me on the inside, and I have a lengthy court process ahead of me.*
>
> *I felt I needed to join in this discussion to get it off my chest. I want his family to know how deeply regretful I am for what I did and that I accept responsibility and know I can never bring him back. I keep thinking of the what ifs, and I can't seem to get them out of my head.*

Like Lisa, it is likely that you are feeling more pain and isolation than you have ever felt before.

Over and over again, those who have unintentionally killed or seriously injured someone come to our Hyacinth Fellowship meetings and tell us it's the first time they have ever talked to another person who's done the same thing, even if their incident was decades ago. Hearing from others who get it is immensely powerful. It can give us strength to free us from this horrible and weighty secret.

As authors, we understand the appeal of keeping our accidents a secret. Maryann didn't tell anyone about hers for 25 years; for Chris, it was two years. But after we started talking about our experiences, we were able to make huge progress in the healing process. And as we shared our situations, people began to approach us with their own stories. A good friend told Maryann that her sister unintentionally killed someone and a neighbor hit a child who was riding a bike. Someone close to Chris told him about a ski patrolman on a snowmobile who struck and killed an 8-year-old skier. Strangers sought us out as well. They wanted to share their own stories and felt safe talking to someone who could understand. As humans, we all have an innate need to share our hurts, but those who unintentionally harm are largely denied the opportunity.

That's why we say that even if you think you don't know any other unintentional killers, you almost certainly do. Every 18 minutes in the United States, someone unintentionally kills another person. That's 82 people a day, 30,000 people a year, not to mention accidents that cause serious injuries, which are much more common.

We live in an accidental world where tragic mistakes are the norm.

While it's difficult to talk about, we are starting to see some positive signs of societal compassion. Slowly but profoundly, this topic is making its way into the light—through news stories, social media, blogs, and other sources. We are doing our best to get the word out about the Hyacinth Fellowship, an organization dedicated to your well-being, bringing compassionate accountability to the challenges of healing and wholeness for those who cause unintentional harm.

The goal of the Fellowship is to build a more compassionate world, one that cares for both victims and perpetrators. Yes, it's controversial. Some people think that those who unintentionally harm should be punished, not pitied, fined, not forgiven. But we have come to realize that our common humanity suffers when ruled by vengeance, retaliation, and division and finds liberation in forgiveness, reconciliation, and restoration. The mission of the Hyacinth Fellowship is about embracing the best of ourselves, defining our life not by a single moment or by our lesser angels but by our better ones.

These convictions led us to establish the Hyacinth Fellowship, a non-profit corporation that will receive all of the profits from this book. The Fellowship supports an emerging community of compassionate people by providing various online support groups, literature, and creative resources. This book is an extension of the Hyacinth mission, providing a handbook to healing and wholeness for people who have caused unintentional harm—and those who care about them.

To help us better understand unintentional harm and how we make our way through it, we've included the actual stories of these events, as written on our Hyacinth blog by those who have committed unintentional harm. While the names have been changed, the stories and the emotions are real—and raw.

Our Four Themes

The handbook is guided by four central themes. Based on our experience, values, beliefs, and sound empirical evidence, these themes are foundational to bringing health and wholeness to those who unintentionally harm.

The first theme is: *You are more than your incident; it does not solely define who you are.*

Our experience and interactions with hundreds of unintentional killers over many years give us a solid cause for optimism. Unintentionally harming someone is awful. It shakes us to our core. But the odds are very good that you can and will feel better. The symptoms that are interfering with your everyday life can almost certainly be managed and will likely subside. You can replace self-castigation and self-contempt with self-understanding and self-compassion. You can regain a sense of belonging and confidence in your own agency and abilities.

You may look back on this time in a few years and realize that, although you will forever carry sorrow and regret about the harm you caused, you are stronger and more compassionate. You can find joy, even if today you are convinced that joy would be an obscenely inappropriate emotion given what has happened.

A few days after Maryann's accident, she had an emergency counseling session with a therapist. She told him she thought the incident would ruin her life and she'd never be the same. He responded with words that have never been forgotten: "You have a choice. You can let this ruin your life, or you can choose to cope and grow." At the time, when she was experiencing all kinds of symptoms and emotions she couldn't control, she didn't feel like she had a choice, but she clung to his words anyway and made growth her goal.

To repeat: this incident does not define who you are. You are the same caring person you were before it happened. What occurred does not mean you are a bad person, even if you were careless or reckless. The very depth of your distress is evidence that you are a caring person. What you did is not the same as who you are.

Our second theme comes from the Buddhist tradition. It is: *There are many paths up the mountain.*

Since your incident, you have likely heard all sorts of random advice: "You have to forgive yourself." "You have to get back on the horse and start riding again." "You have to move on." "You have to try EMDR." "You have to come to Jesus." "You didn't intend harm, so you don't need to feel guilty." "You have to..."

People are full of well-meaning advice. At a time when you may be questioning your own judgment—after all, look what happened—it is tempting to let others tell you what to do.

There are two problems with this approach. First, their well-meaning advice might not be good advice for you; what works for one person may not be helpful to another. The second problem is that part of healing and recovery is regaining a sense of your own agency and control.

In the immediate aftermath of your incident, you may not be thinking clearly. You probably need to consult friends and family about important decisions and choices. You've been traumatized. You are not well. Yes, over time, you need to be in charge, you need to discover your own truth in your healing and recovery, but that's not now.

This is what we mean by "many paths up the mountain." This principle acknowledges that we may all strive to reach the same summit— peace with ourselves and our world—but we will undoubtedly take different paths to get there. Some will be more difficult than others. Some people can come to terms with the incident rather quickly; for others, it can take a very, very long time. Sometimes the path is steep but short; sometimes, it takes longer but has a gentler slope. Sometimes we will encounter unexpected obstacles and have to retrace our steps and try again. But eventually, we will get there. Or perhaps find that our journey is its own destination. You are moving toward self-healing and self-discovery. It's not a race. Hurrying won't help. And it's up to each of us to find the path that works best for us.

Even though we are convinced that the journey to healing will be different for each person, we also have some serious recommendations. First, seek psychotherapy. Find someone who's experienced. We don't recommend any single approach or modality because that depends on you, but we do urge you to seek evidence-based help.

Secondly, using alcohol or non-prescription drugs to help you cope is not the answer. This behavior will nearly always make things worse. And if you engage in self-harming behavior, like cutting, or thinking about suicide, this is a sure sign that you have lost the path and need some help finding your way.

Our third theme is: *The burden we carry is psychological, physical, and spiritual.*

Our experience has shown that while we naturally seek professionals to help us heal our minds and bodies, we also need to tend to our souls. We have come to believe there is something at work beyond us that plays a role in our health and well-being—something spiritual.

While our spiritual and religious beliefs differ widely from individual to individual, our experience suggests that drawing on these convictions makes a difference. In fact, your accident may be serving as a vehicle of spiritual awakening that can be used to help you better cope with what has happened.

Unintentional killing unwittingly transforms us. It can plunge us into a depth of suffering we have never known before. It can put us in touch with feelings and people we had never known before. But suffering is often a crucible of creativity and positive transformation. It can give us an occasion to grow in our understanding of ourselves and our world.

We believe that we cannot pull ourselves out of our pain by ourselves, that we need someone, something beyond us, a higher power or other spiritual anchor, to call upon to help. We believe our path to healing involves surrender, forgiveness, and ultimately transformation.

If you have spiritual or religious beliefs, you can call upon them and integrate them with the material here. If not, stick with the psychological level of understanding but try to be open to the possibility of something more.

Our fourth theme is: *Embrace compassionate accountability.*

We live in a world that is quick to judge, quick to jump to conclusions, quick to condemn, and quick to sentence. Our approach is almost always to slow down this default setting. We believe in accountability, but we also believe in the compassionate exercise of it. You have been beaten up enough in your mind and probably by the circumstances surrounding your events, and while accountability is needed, so is compassion.

We need to remember that compassion without accountability is empty, but accountability without compassion is cruel. We need both.

Accountability means accepting the simple fact that, despite the best of intentions, we killed or seriously injured someone. That incident has all kinds of ripple effects, many of which we will never know. It needs to be given its due. We need to think about why this happened, what, if anything, we need to change about our own behavior and choices, and what steps we want to take toward making some of those changes. We need to consider what this death or injury means to us.

This does not mean heaping blame on ourselves. It does not mean harsh self-punishment. It means using our rational minds to explore what we could and couldn't control and to address what is under our control. We can control our own behavior, of course, although we might need help in some cases such as substance abuse. We can also control the meaning we choose to make of this accident and our response to death or injury; we can decide how to honor the experience.

Compassion means treating ourselves the way we would treat a friend or family member under similar circumstances. We would offer empathy, kindness, and love. We would not tell them they were horrible human beings. We would not snap at them to get over it. We deserve compassion because we are human beings who care and who are suffering. And we deserve compassion because it has practical benefits, including helping us regain our lives as parents, spouses, friends, workers, and community members.

Our Roadmap

With these four overarching themes in mind, here's where we'll go.

Chapter One gives us the lay of the land, examining the scope of unintentional harm, assuring us that our feelings are normal, and reminding us that no matter how deep the trauma, odds are we can find a way to greater peace and self-acceptance.

Chapters Two and Three takes us through the "anatomy of an unintentional killing." We break down fatal, unintentional events into two parts: the early stage and the latter stage. We learn about acute stress and PTSD as we begin to understand why we feel the way we do.

Chapter Four introduces us to the concept of moral injury. When we unintentionally kill, we violate our moral compass. We are not meant to harm others with impunity, so we feel guilt, regret, and mental torment when we unintentionally harm. While our physical health may be fine, our souls are unwell.

Chapter Five examines spirituality and trauma. Personal spirituality can offer a wellspring of coping tools and mechanisms that have proven to enhance healing. Practices like prayer, meditation, and giving back can be sturdy foundations for our recovery.

Chapter Six offers coping tools, specifically self-care. We examine appropriate therapeutic options and medications. Everyone who unintentionally kills or seriously harms needs to see a psychotherapist who is able to ground and guide us through the tragedies. We'll also touch on self-help tools like writing, meditation, and peer support.

Chapter Seven explores the dynamics of helping someone who has unintentionally harmed. We'll look at the important questions such as: What do we say? How do we act? How can we best walk alongside someone who's hurting in this unique way?

Chapter Eight introduces the possibility of hope. Every event in life, no matter how tragic, can offer insight, growth, and transformation. As the adage goes, "Don't waste your suffering." Amidst the feelings of isolation and sadness, we will ask the question: "What new thing is being done in us that could only have come about on this path?"

This final chapter is devoted to encouragement. We have known many people and heard many stories, and the examples of people rebuilding their lives are remarkably encouraging. Humans are incredibly resilient and resourceful. Many people have unintentionally harmed and found ways to live full and productive lives. Why should we be any different?

Throughout these chapters, we will share real-life stories. They are disturbing and tragic. We have included them not to shock and titillate but to speak truth and strengthen our community. The human journey, while beautiful and happy, is also filled with shocking events and horrible occurrences.

If at any time as you are reading, you start to feel overwhelmed by harmful thoughts or emotions, simply put the book down for a while. You may want to try some of the exercises for grounding and mindfulness we'll mention in Chapter Six. Some of the material can be retraumatizing, especially if your feelings are raw. You might want to read this book with a friend or relative, bring it to therapy, or take it in small bites.

Also, our book is not a substitute for psychotherapy or counseling. We cannot say this enough: if you have unintentionally harmed someone, please seek professional help. There are low-cost options for therapy if that's a concern but make therapy a priority. If you think you don't deserve help, do it for those who care about you, or do it so that you can manage the stress you are under enough to be of service to others and to help create safer, kinder, more caring communities.

If you are feeling suicidal or thinking about harming yourself, please get immediate help. You can call the Suicide Prevention Hotline at 988, go to a local emergency room, call your doctor or therapist, or contact a community mental health clinic and tell them you're in crisis.

There is help for your pain.

Suicide is not the answer to your distress, and we believe your pain will lessen, especially if you follow the exercises in this book and seek counseling.

Our hope is that by learning more about unintentional killing and injury you may find solace. You may find healing.

You may find yourself.

We believe you can emerge from this painful time stronger and more compassionate, manifesting what psychologists call post-traumatic growth. We know this is possible because not only are we going through this ourselves, but we've spent years talking, corresponding, and counseling others who have unintentionally killed someone. We've seen how resilient we are and how we can heal and even grow through this.

You can too.

Now, here are our stories.

Maryann's Story

My accident happened in 1977 when I was a 22-year-old student. On a beautiful spring day, an 8-year-old boy named Brian ran in front of my car on a rural highway. He died before he reached the hospital.

Right away, I had many symptoms of acute and post-traumatic stress: intrusive images and flashbacks, inability to concentrate, sometimes feeling numb, and other times overwhelmed with tremendous grief and fear. When I tried to drive, I hallucinated people on the road and slammed on my brakes in traffic. Obviously, that was dangerous, so I gave up my car and didn't drive for close to two years.

The worst part was the guilt and shame I felt. No one blamed me for Brian's death, but that didn't stop me from blaming myself. I told myself that one of my punishments for killing a child was that I should never have children of my own. Mostly, I was scared I would hurt or kill someone else. I withdrew from other people and spent a lot of time by myself. I did not allow myself to feel happy, proud, or excited—as soon as I would start to feel happy, I would be flooded with horrific memories and images.

The adults around me—parents, professors, a therapist, and other relatives—were sympathetic and helpful, but they all advised me to simply move on with my life. "It's so sad, but it's not your fault," they said. "You have your whole life ahead of you." That sounded reasonable to me, but I found myself unable to move on. I thought about the accident, the child, and his family constantly. I didn't want to admit that I was struggling, so I faked it. I told people I was doing well and tried to act like my idea of a "normal" 22-year-old.

This divide between the "real" me and the "fake" me continued for about 20 years. A few years after the accident, I moved to California, and once there, I stopped talking about it. Even my husband didn't know the story. We never had children. I focused on my career and worked long hours.

This fake life started to change in 2003. I had begun therapy the year before to address depression and anxiety. It didn't take long before I started to talk to my therapist about the accident and all of the unresolved trauma and guilt. That summer, an elderly man lost control of his car at the Santa Monica Farmer's Market, killing 10 and injuring over 60 people. This terrible tragedy dominated the news for days. As I watched the coverage, it hurt to hear people calling him a murderer and their assumption that he had killed and injured so many people on purpose. I felt compelled to speak up on his behalf and after 20 years of silence, I ended up telling my story on a brief radio commentary.

All of a sudden, my accident was no longer a secret. I was fortunate that I received lots of support for speaking out. As I continued to write and speak about what it's like to unintentionally kill someone, others who had done the same thing sought me out. Until these conversations, most of us had never talked to anyone else who had unintentionally killed or injured someone. Each of us had to figure out how to cope on our own.

As part of my own process of making amends, I decided I did not want others to suffer all alone after unintentionally killing or injuring someone. I had lived a small, constrained life for many years because I was too sad, afraid, and guilty to spread my wings. Instead of taking risks to make the world a better place, I played it safe. When I finally stopped hiding, I found so much more energy and had so much more to give.

I created a modest website that I called Accidental Impacts. Slowly, people found their way to it. Some years later, Chris Yaw, some others, and I formed a nonprofit corporation, which is now called the Hyacinth Fellowship. Today, the organization reaches thousands of people every year, offers a variety of programs, and is a valuable resource for those who have caused unintentional harm and death. When we support one another, we are better able to overcome adversity.

Chris's Story

The worst day of my life?

Easy. Saturday, November 9, 2013.

That's when I hired Kenny to rake up the leaves in my yard. A lifelong postal worker in Detroit, Kenny had just retired and was looking forward to building his landscape business and spending time with his children and grandchildren.

None of that would ever happen because of a decision I made five years earlier to install a garage door opener in my 1926 Tudor home on the cheap. The existing doors were solid oak, weighed hundreds of pounds, and required a commercial motor to open and close. The unit was void of the usual, residential safety features. The installer told me these would be expensive. So, I said yes to the opener but balked at the additional safety features.

On that horrible fall morning, Kenny showed up for work, but he broke his rake and asked if he could borrow mine. I went to the garage to fetch one, showed him where the garden tools were kept, and then asked him to return the rake when he was finished. Around midday, I discovered Kenny had become tangled in the doors. He had been pinned there for some time. Months later, the medical examiner concluded he'd been crushed.

As my wife called 911, I lowered his cold, lifeless body to the cement driveway. As a minister, my first instinct was to offer prayers for Kenny, Last Rites as some call it, before covering him and waiting for the police. When they arrived, they camped out well into the night as medical examiners, police detectives, and Kenny's family visited in small waves.

I remember little else than being stunned. I was in a fog, like I was living in a horrible nightmare. How could this be happening? A man killed on our property? A family eternally devastated because of my negligence? Would we be criminally charged? Would we be sued?

Would we go broke paying for my tragic mistake? These feelings went on for months. I started smoking. I lost 40 pounds. My 10-year marriage ended.

Soon after Kenny's death, my son and I attended his funeral, and 12 months after that, we were sued. Our insurance company agreed to pay a modest settlement to Kenny's family to settle things. I wish they could have received more.

Getting through the aftermath of this incident took a combination of psychotherapy, spirituality, and community.

I relied upon prayer, community, and professional guidance to aright my capsized life. I leaned heavily upon my friends and faith community to help me deal with the overwhelming feelings of guilt, blame, and sorrow. And my therapist talked some good sense into me. My feelings, while greatly lessened, still persisted.

A few years later, I stumbled upon a magazine article about Maryann and her organization, and we became fast friends. She graciously invited me to write for the blog, and we started the foundation and various outreach activities.

While I can't bring Kenny back, I can allow him to inspire me. I can listen for his voice. I can imagine his words to me. I can work to brighten the world, as he did. I like to think that the work I now do to speak, write, counsel, and organize people who've done things like this is bringing a smile to his face. I like to think that he would not want me to forget about him or others who suffer through things like this. I like to think he would want me to use his death to bring life to others.

CHAPTER ONE

Hyacinths in Bloom

Here's a typical visitor post from our website:

My story is unusual, different. I watched as a small child in my care was run over and killed by a riding lawnmower. I was 19. I am now 66. Many people in my life do not know this story. Some do. I don't believe I ever processed this. I have felt unbearable guilt that my negligence allowed this to happen. I was almost charged with criminal negligence. People tell me I was very young, but that does not take away the guilt.

I get through life by pushing this memory down deep inside me. I still work with children, which you may think is strange. I have a master's degree in early childhood education. I have three children of my own. How are these things possible?

Those of you who killed someone purely by accident, not because you were reckless, not because you were not paying attention, not because you didn't see the danger, you can't really know the depth of guilt that I feel. Whenever I begin to think about it, I want to rerun the tape so I will stop it from happening. I have suffered from terrible depression all my life. I had serious emotional difficulties as a child and then this happened. To be honest, I'm not sure why I looked for the site or why I am even writing this. —Roy

Roy has three things in common with others who unintentionally harm. First, he thinks his story is unique. Second, he's coping with it by ignoring it. And third, he hasn't told many people. His is a common response to a very common occurrence.

Unintentional Harm Happens All the Time

Roy probably thinks his story is rare because he's never known anyone who's done the same thing. Sure, he may have heard of an incident here and there, but he doesn't think he knows anyone in the same situation.

Unintentional harm is a hidden occurrence. We have had many instances when friends or coworkers will learn that we've unintentionally killed and say, "I didn't know! Why didn't you tell me?" The fact is we are ashamed, embarrassed, and deeply troubled. Our stories are horrible and often triggering. No one should be surprised that this topic isn't often breached at cocktail parties.

One of the worst things about killing someone in an accident is that you can never talk about it openly for fear of judgment or worse. It's not socially acceptable to have run someone over. People always think you are somehow to blame, even if they don't say it. It's hard not being able to share your trauma like it's shameful and somehow a crime. —Robert

It is hard to quantify the exact number of people who have caused unintentional harm or death. There is no central database, there is no public or private entity keeping tabs on unintentional harm or death. Perhaps this subject has not garnered enough interest or attention to merit such tabulation. However, we have assembled some data points to come up with a reasonable estimate.

- About 28,000 drivers each year survive a crash in which at least one person died. Of these, about 6,000 drivers hit and kill pedestrians and 750 kill bicyclists. The remaining 21,000 collide with other motor vehicles, and we don't know how many fit the criteria to be unintentional killers.

- Estimates of fatalities from medical errors vary from about 25,000 deaths per year in the U.S. to about 100,000 deaths per year. The number of providers who perceive themselves to be unintentional killers is entirely unknown, and deaths due to medical errors by non-medical professionals (such as people caring for family members) is similarly unknown.

- The Center for Disease Control reports that unintentional shootings kill an average of 500 people in the U.S. each year.

- On average, about 400 children under the age of 15 drown each year, with two-thirds younger than 5 years old (U.S. Consumer Product Safety Commission). In many of these situations, the adults responsible for supervising the children are likely to consider themselves to be unintentional killers.

- On average, two children in the U.S. die every day from burns, and another two die every day from unintentional poisoning. A significant percentage of their parents or caregivers are likely to consider themselves unintentional killers.

- Nearly 40 children per year in the U.S. die of heat stroke from being closed inside a hot car (National Safety Council). Most of the drivers would consider themselves unintentional killers.

- More than a million people died of COVID-19 in the U.S. alone. Even if only a small percentage of those who transmitted COVID to someone who died define themselves as unintentional killers, this might be the most frequent type of unintentional killing, at least in the last few years.

Based on these numbers, we conservatively estimate that 30,000 people unintentionally kill someone in the U.S. each year. That's one person unintentionally killed every 18 minutes.

It's important to note that none of these data points include unintentional killings like Chris's, which occurred at a private home, did not result in criminal charges, and was not chronicled in any sort of media.

Another helpful resource could be generated by psychologists and therapists who treat people who have caused unintentional harm— but there's currently no such database. And, as we see in Roy's case, many, if not most, of those who unintentionally kill do not seek counseling.

If we include those who unintentionally cause serious injury, the numbers go up at least tenfold, keeping in mind this data is even more incomplete and more unreliable for injuries compared to deaths.

Our point is that there are lots of people who have unintentionally harmed. You may feel alone, but you are not.

Two weeks ago, I was on my way to work very early in the dark. I collided with a man on a motorcycle. He died last week. I am all over the place emotionally and trying to hold it together. I'll be fine for a little while and function like normal at work, but once my mind isn't engaged elsewhere, it's all I think about. The man had a child and one on the way. My husband won't listen to me say anything about feeling guilty or to blame; he just gets angry. This is only just beginning, and I feel all alone. —Pamela

---

The Hyacinth Fellowship

In Greek mythology, a character named Hyacinth was the fatal victim of unintentional harm. It is said that the blood from his wounds fell to the ground, causing the bloom of the hyacinth, one of most fragrant and beautiful of garden flowers.

In facing the horror, pain, and shame of unintentional harm, we offer this image as a name to describe this phenomenon. The hyacinth is our symbol of hope after harm, beauty out of suffering, and an aspirational icon for those of us who have done the unimaginable.

If you have unintentionally caused serious injury, pain, or death, we consider you to be a member of the Hyacinth Fellowship. This means you answered "yes" to the following three questions:

First, were you involved in an incident in which another person was seriously injured or killed? Often that incident is a sudden event like a car crash, but it can also be less violent, like transmitting COVID or making a medical mistake. These incidents can be something you did, like unintentionally shooting someone, or they can be something you didn't do, like not noticing a toddler had fallen into your swimming pool.

Second, do you consider yourself to be responsible for the fatality or injury? Responsibility does not necessarily mean you believe yourself to be culpable or at fault for the damage done. Rather, it means you believe yourself to have been the agent of harm. For instance, Maryann was unable to avoid hitting a child who darted into the road in front of her car. She was not legally to blame nor civilly liable, but she considers herself responsible for the fatality because she was at the wheel.

Note that others might consider you responsible, but it's you who must see yourself that way. For instance, a grieving family might accuse a doctor of inappropriate treatment that led to the patient's death, but the doctor may disagree, believing the treatment was reasonable and the fatality was inevitable. The doctor is not a Hyacinth Fellowship member.

It also doesn't matter if other people do not hold you responsible for the fatality or injury. What matters is how you perceive yourself.

There's one exception here. Sometimes people hold themselves responsible for another person's misfortune without any rational basis. For instance, we heard from a schizophrenic young man who believed that his thoughts could kill. We also received a request for help from a daughter who believed that the daily vitamin she had recommended to her mother caused her mother's death. Because these perceptions are not tethered to reality, such individuals are not Fellowship members.

Third, were your intentions good or at least benign? This one seems obvious: if you intended harm, or if you showed callous disregard for others' well-being, you are not a Fellowship member. For instance, one legal scholar gave an example of someone throwing a brick out of a window twenty stories above a big crowd. They might not have wanted to kill someone, but they obviously didn't care much if they did. That person is not a Fellowship member. (If, on the other hand, they were trying to move the brick and unintentionally dropped it, they would be.)

If you answered yes to all three questions, you are a member of the Hyacinth Fellowship.

The Hyacinth Fellowship Definition

Involved in an incident in which another person was seriously injured or killed

Consider yourself responsible for the fatality or injury

Did not intend harm

It bears repeating: some Fellowship members are blameless, while others made serious mistakes or were negligent or even reckless. They are likely to have different experiences and different needs, but they are all members of the Fellowship.

Unintentional Harm Has Distinctions

As unintended students of this subject, we have learned that accidental killing harms us deeply. We've seen it lead to failed relationships, poor job performance, and addiction. In some cases, it leads to post-traumatic stress disorder, or PTSD, which is a mental health disorder caused by very stressful, frightening, or distressing events.

And, as we've noted, unintentionally harming someone brings distinctive challenges all its own.

First, there is the moral component, the way so many Fellowship members are mired in guilt and shame and feel undeserving of solace or support. Later we will learn that this is called moral injury. It is different from PTSD; you can have one without the other. But when they occur together, as is the case for so many in our Fellowship, the recovery process is complicated and complex. Psychologists have seen this combination before, especially in military settings with soldiers who unintentionally kill civilians or kill their own comrades through friendly fire, for instance. But it is less common (or less recognized) in civilian populations and less understood as well.

A second distinctive element of unintentional harm is the way others judge us. The victim's friends, family, and communities, shocked by the loss of one of their own, may lash out in anger and seek retaliation, either inside or outside of the courts. This includes trolling someone on social media or even physically attacking them. On top of that, we know judgments made by community members and others are subject to certain cognitive errors or bias, so they are more likely to mistakenly assume intentionality and/or assume the Fellowship member should have or could have known better. Of course, in some situations, we may have been negligent or careless, but that is much different than committing intentional murder, which is what some people may believe.

These judgements are particularly prone to be erroneous under certain circumstances, such as when the event sparks horror and emotional distress; when making snap judgments with limited information; or when race, ethnicity, nationality, social class, or gender differs from the person doing the judging.

Nonetheless, these perceptions are painful and sometimes traumatic in and of themselves. To the extent Fellowship members are regarded as perpetrators, their needs are likely to be dismissed or even belittled. One might hear, "Don't try to turn yourself into a victim." To be clear: Hyacinth Fellowship members are not the victims. When unintentional death or serious injury happens, our first concern is for the victims and their loved ones. They are usually innocent themselves and are rightly the first to whom we give attention, aid, sympathy, and support. However, Fellowship members still carry tremendous emotional burdens of guilt, shame, embarrassment, and isolation because some people can have little empathy for those who have done what we've done.

A third way unintentional killing differs from other traumas is that there is a monumental lack of resources. Academic journals, the web, bookstores, and mainstream media are full of information and first-person accounts of so many traumas: childhood abuse, domestic violence, sexual or other assaults, natural disasters, mass shootings or terrorism, and so forth, a litany of human misery and suffering. But there is hardly anything about or for those who unintentionally kill or injure someone, apart from a few memoirs, a couple of podcasts, and a single website. In an exhaustive literature search Maryann conducted for an academic paper, she found only two articles about unintentional killing in the psychological literature. One was more than 10 years old, and the other, over 30 years old. A lack of study indicates a lack of interest, which is one reason members of our Fellowship tend to feel alone. One of our goals with the Fellowship is to provide a host of resources on our website, www.hyacinthfellowship.org.

I know that many people have experienced terrible tragedies in life. Being a nurse makes me even more acutely aware of that. And I am a fairly open person with people I know well, but even after all these years, I've only told a couple of very trusted co-workers about my accident. It's the one thing that I just don't really talk about that much. Looking back at my life, I've always felt like the more time I place between when it happened and myself, the more "removed" I will be from it or something. It's hard to explain, but lately I am realizing it's just not true. —Ruth

---

A Good Funeral

In Ancient Greece, the term *lethe* meant "to hide" or "to cover." Alethia, then, meant "to uncover," which leads to Alethia's meaning in contemporary Greek: "truth," that which is uncovered. Lethe is what we tend to do with our trauma; we hide or even bury it. We want to treat it as an "untruth"—something that is not "us," So, we bury it. But there are two ways to approach this burial.

The first is to put the horrendous event out of sight as fast as possible. We dig a hole, dump it in, and fill it as soon as we can. We don't take time for talk, reflection, or processing. Certainly, we would never put up a marker. We don't ever want to find it, much less visit it again. What's been done has been done, let's wash our hands, do our best to forget, and turn our attention to something else as quickly as possible.

The second option is to consider this burial a funeral. This is a "good burial." A funeral is an intentional bookend to a difficult, even devastating time that is done with grace and thoughtfulness. A funeral does not erase or gloss over pain but puts it into perspective, acknowledging the pain for what it is and what it can bring about. At funerals, we have the opportunity to do the healthy, ongoing, and very human work of mourning, remembering, and letting go.

Good funerals help us acknowledge important truths. We look into the casket and see that which has affected us. We own up to the reality of what's there. We weep with sorrow.

We also confirm the reality of what remains: our resilience, the presence of caring people who help us, and the reality of our higher power to help us frame the event with grace and strengthen us for what's ahead.

Finally, with good funerals, we put up markers, not simply as a way to hold on but as a way to let go. There's an anniversary. There's a life that mattered. There's a milestone we've passed, even a challenge we've met, when we can remember that the tragedy we brought about has shaped and molded us into who we are today. And no matter what we've done, we are loved, we are valuable, and we have work we can do to better the world.

We hope this book can help you design a good funeral.

Key Takeaways

* An estimated 30,000 people accidentally kill someone each year. But few people talk about it, keeping silent out of shame, guilt, embarrassment, or any number of emotions. But you are not alone. The Hyacinth Fellowship was created as a place for support and help for those who unintentionally killed or seriously harmed someone.

* Unintentional harm has some distinct challenges, including moral injury and judgment from others. This book offers insight and strategies for dealing with the aftermath of being an accidental killer and strategies for coping and healing.

Discussion Questions

1. Do you feel alone in your experience as an accidental killer? Were you surprised to learn than an estimated 30,000 people accidentally kill each year? What is your response to this number?

2. Do you talk about the incident to others? What is keeping you quiet? How do you think others would respond if they knew about the incident?

3. The authors end the chapter with the idea of "A Good Funeral." In what ways do you think this approach could help you with healing? What truths do you need to acknowledge?

CHAPTER TWO

The Anatomy of an Unintentional Killing: The Early Stages

I killed somebody today. She died at the hospital, but it's all the same. I tried to stop but failed to in time. She just darted out in front of me. Lord, forgive me please. I know I won't forgive myself. I don't think i can ever be behind the wheel again. I am just.... angry. Why here? There is nothing I will learn from this, is there? I was sober and working. Then I ended a life. I am so disconnected from this, it horrifies me. I just keep seeing her roll over my hood and the blood on the asphalt in my head. No break. No commercials. Just death. Over and over. —Ali

The minutes before the police arrived at the accident scene were the worst minutes of my life. I don't remember all of it, but I do remember the sense of horror and terror gripping me. I was feral in those minutes, worried about my own survival, convinced the knot of witnesses and others would kill me if they found me. And even as I shook with fear, I kept picturing the moment of impact. He was just a little boy. So fragile. I spent hours at the accident scene while the police investigated. They told me the child had died. I rode wave after wave of grief, guilt, shock, and fear. And then I was home, and all I could think about was what happened— there was a slideshow constantly playing in my mind with one horrible image after another. I was afraid to leave my apartment. I went from tears of grief to trembling in fear to shameful moments of rage at the child for running in front of my car. And hours would go by, and I had no idea how the time passed or what I'd been doing. —Ellen

In the immediate aftermath of an unintentional killing, most of us are traumatized. Our adrenaline is pumping. Our minds are racing. All sense of time is lost. Horrid images play and replay across the movie screens of our minds in endless and unstoppable loops as we try to piece together what happened. For most of us, it's the worst experience of our lives.

Days after a notable unintentional shooting involving actor Alec Baldwin in 2021, Maryann sat down with host Jada Pinkett-Smith as a guest on her talk show. Maryann was asked about the healing journey. "What does that look like?" Jada asked. Maryann looked her in the eye and said without reservation, "Job number one is getting trauma under control."

Maryann discusses trauma recovery with actress and activist Jada Pinkett Smith on her show, Red Table Talk.
(Credit: Red Table Talk)

In Chapters 2 and 3, we will unpack what we call the early and latter stages of trauma and offer some advice to help you get through them.

The early stages include the hours and days immediately following our incidents. What did we do? Whom did we call? What did we say? We've included a worksheet at the end of this chapter to help you gather your thoughts, make initial plans, and begin to set a course. We advise you to work through this form sooner rather than later.

The early stages are about reaction. It's a time of confusion and uncertain navigation: how we initially react is often beyond our control.

The latter stages encompass all subsequent time. How are we coming down from the adrenaline of this event? How are we making sense of things? How are we carving out an afterlife? This is no longer about reaction; it's about response. Here, we get to choose. Here, we have the opportunity to regain our sense of control.

As we react and respond to our event, we discover that we may behave in ways we never have before, saying and doing things we've never done and may not even understand. It's because we're going through a thing called trauma.

You and Your Trauma

One way to think of trauma is by thinking about professional auto racing.

Of course, there are thrills, excitement, and bragging rights at stake. But another reason some sponsors are involved in professional racing is because it can offer an unparalleled and fertile field to improve vehicle safety. Bumpers, metals, plastics, and safety harnesses are just a few of the many components of modern passenger cars that were either invented or perfected on the race track.

When a car crashes at high speeds, perhaps by taking a turn badly or clipping a competitor's car, a rather dramatic episode unfurls: as the car rolls, side panels fly off, wheels roll away, and the dashboard detaches, a sturdy roll cage emerges, protecting its precious cargo inside. Oftentimes, we marvel when the driver pops out of the wreckage and walks away, seemingly unscathed.

That roll cage—inconspicuous and unnoticed when the car is all together—is suddenly revealed as a lifesaver and critical component.

That roll cage is our trauma response.

By definition, trauma response is a set of adaptive responses rooted in our biology or primitive biology, and it's there to keep us safe.

Trauma researcher MaryCatherine McDonald says that our bodies are made to cope with trauma. For centuries, we've been taught that being traumatized means we are somehow broken—and that trauma only happens to people who are too fragile or flawed to deal with hardship. Instead, McDonald says, the trauma response proves our spirit cannot be broken. We are wired to respond to trauma in healthy ways. Our response is wonderfully crafted to secure, protect, and equip us to come out of our experiences.

So, the changes in your pulse, sleep habits, appetite, and other aspects of your physiology and personality should be examined through the lens of your trauma. Depending on your unique wiring, this can take a variety of forms. One common development is acute trauma disorder.

Acute Stress Disorder

According to the American Psychiatric Association, when we experience or witness "actual or threatened death [or] serious injury," we are at risk of acute stress disorder. To fully meet this diagnosis, an individual must show nine or more of the symptoms listed below. These symptoms must be severe enough to interfere with social, work, family, or other areas of functioning.

Acute Stress Disorder Symptoms

In the immediate aftermath of your event, you may experience these general symptoms:

- Recurrent, involuntary, and intrusive distressing memories of the traumatic event

- Recurrent distressing dreams in which the content and/or affect of the dream are related to the event

- Persistent inability to experience positive emotions

Symptoms of a dissociative nature:

- An altered sense of the reality of one's surroundings or oneself (e.g., seeing oneself from another's perspective, being in a daze, time slowing).

- Inability to remember an important aspect of the traumatic event

Symptoms of avoidance:

- Efforts to avoid distressing memories, thoughts, or feelings about the traumatic event

- Efforts to avoid external reminders (people, places, conversations, activities, objects, situations) that arouse distressing memories, thoughts, or feelings about the traumatic event

Symptoms of arousal:

- Sleep disturbance
- Irritable behavior and angry outbursts (with little or no provocation)
- Hypervigilance
- Problems with concentration
- Exaggerated startle response

Acute stress disorder can be diagnosed anytime between three days and one month after the traumatic event.

If you are experiencing any of the symptoms of acute stress disorder, keep in mind that they are a normal response to an abnormal situation. We couldn't avoid our incident, and we couldn't save the victim, and now we can't avoid the intrusive images, sense of depersonalization, emotional distress, startle reactions, and other symptoms that interfere with our ability to function normally.

The irony of our severe distress is that it comes at a very bad time.

The immediate aftermath of our incident is when we need to function effectively. This is when we are forced to deal with family members, police, lawyers, insurance companies, doctors or other health care providers, etc. We face crucial decisions about how to manage our responsibilities, and we must make important choices, such as whether to retain an attorney, how to find a therapist, or who we can count on for support. Acute stress disorder doesn't help matters. So, let's look at some way we can help manage our response.

Coping with the Immediate Aftermath: Phone a Friend

I went home and told my parents what happened, and they were shocked and could not believe what happened. I went to my room, and I could not get out of bed. I kept thinking about the crash over and over and over again. I am diagnosed with OCD, anxiety, and depression, and they were all turned up to ten. I was in my bed for almost eighteen hours, and my mom was worried and talked to me the next morning. I felt horrible. I could not believe that I did something so foolish. I kept wishing that I could go back in time and actually pay attention to my surroundings more and see that there was a cyclist who was crossing the street. I felt so bad for the man, for his family, for the pain that I caused. Since then, I cannot get it out of my head. I am taking a summer class at my local college, and it is impossible to study. I can't think normally, and my sleep schedule has been all over the place. I feel so guilty, so ashamed, and so stupid for what I did. I am so nervous when I drive now, and I am worried that I am going to do something like this again. It's the guilt that is tearing me apart, and I keep getting flashbacks of the whole event. I don't know what to do. I'm so scared and frightened by all of this. I feel like I will never be able to get over this and that I will have to live with this guilt for the rest of my life, and I'm only 22. —Cassandra

After your incident, you need caring emotional support. This can come from family, friends, neighbors, therapists, clergy, you name it. Seek it first. Call a friend.

There are also numerous practical issues that need attention as well. Here, a friend can be invaluable as well. If you had a car crash, you need to deal with the insurance agency. If your car is drivable or if you are unable to drive, you need to plan for transportation. You may have to deal with the police or prosecutor's office. If yours was a particularly newsworthy event, there might be media contacting you or social media accounts that need attention. You may need time away from work or school. Some people may need to be informed about what happened.

How we deal with these issues is a delicate balancing act. On the one hand, trauma can interfere with concentration, logic, and sound decision-making. On the other hand, part of our healing involves regaining a sense of agency and control.

We recommend that you sort through friends and family members to find the person or people who can help you think. These are the people who can listen to you with compassion, disagree respectfully, reason clearly, and help you make a plan.

Those who help may be a spouse or a parent unless they, too, are traumatized. You will likely need more than one person to hold you while you cry, run a few errands, or help you find a great therapist or lawyer. All of these kinds of support (and more) are useful and valuable and mean a great deal. We encourage you to call on friends and family and gratefully accept the solace and help they offer. You will likely find that this task requires a combination of problem-solving and listening skills.

Whoever it is, sit down with them and go through the checklist at the end of this chapter. For each item, fill in the action item, the person who will help, and when this needs to be done.

You may need to do this more than once, as your needs evolve. But going through this process will begin to give you a sense of control over your life. And it will help you cope with practical issues so you can focus more of your energy on your psychological and spiritual well-being.

We realize that you may be thinking, "I can't follow this advice because I don't want to tell anyone what happened." As we've mentioned, after our incidents, most of us want to hide or withdraw. We don't want to upset family and friends. We are deeply ashamed. We are afraid of being blamed. And we don't feel deserving of sympathy or support.

Even though it's upsetting and scary and makes it more real to tell someone what happened, you need and deserve support at this time. Take a big breath and figure out who can help you think. Then take another big breath and talk to them. It may be the first of many difficult steps that can help you move through this situation.

Consult a Therapist

An off-duty firefighter asked me if I was okay, and I responded, "I just hit a child with my car. I am not okay." I have only told my mother about it, and she lives far away from me. I don't know how I will find out how the girl is doing. I don't know how I can go on if I killed her. I don't want to tell anyone else I know because I don't want them to look at me differently, to feel sorry for me, or to see me as a monster who hit a kid. I don't deserve their feeling bad for me, and I can't handle the alternative. I don't know what will happen next. I want to know how she is and what this will lead to legally and financially for me. I want to know the outcome so I can know how guilty I need to feel so that I can start paying for it. I just keep thinking of the moment when I hit her. I screamed. I wanted nothing to be real. I want this to not have happened.
—Michael

The tailspin most of us go into following our incidents has us begging for a soft landing. This is where therapists can help.

While there is no single formula for coping, we have learned that, as tough as it is in most cases, consulting a professional counselor is the most helpful way to process our experiences. By investing upfront in counseling, you will cope more effectively, you will relieve the burden placed on yourself and your family, and you will receive compassion and practical guidance.

That is not to say it will be easy. A therapist will not show you how to "get over it," but in those first few weeks, he or she will help you manage distress or trauma symptoms, explore your beliefs and feelings about the accident, offer solace and empathy, and help you think through decisions and plans.

Depending on the constellation of your family relationships and the depth of harm you're experiencing, you may consider including your significant other or wider family at some point. What affects us affects those around us, and sometimes they can benefit from the expert advice from therapists.

Consult an Attorney

Because we live in such a complex, litigious society, we generally advise retaining a lawyer. This does not mean that you are guilty of anything; it does not mean that you are being over-protective of yourself or insensitive to the victim; and it does not mean that you are inviting conflict or discord. To the extent that criminal charges or a civil lawsuit are possibilities, however, you are entering a new world full of processes, procedures, regulations, and requirements that are strange and complex—and can have major effects on you and your family.

Ask friends, do a web search, and don't be afraid to interview attorneys who have experience in the type of incident in which you were involved. Find someone you trust and with whom you feel comfortable. Attorneys can be very helpful not just in navigating the legal and civil issues that may be at play but also in serving as helpful intermediaries when it comes to making contact with the victim's family and others.

Call Your Insurance Company

You may be surprised at the extent of your insurance coverage when it comes to causing unintentional harm. In some cases, like an auto crash, this is obvious. But incidents at home and at work may also be covered. Make the call, consult your agent, and review your coverage as soon as you can.

If you've retained an attorney, all the better. A good lawyer will explain what is happening or what might happen and work with you to determine how best to respond.

Under certain circumstances, you may be told that your insurance company will represent your interests. This usually works out fine. But keep in mind that the insurance company's priority is itself. And our insurers are used to working alongside personal lawyers to ensure the best possible result. While in many cases, our interests and the insurance company align; if they don't, having your own attorney as an advocate can be important.

Practice Self-Care

In the immediate aftermath of your incident, try to be intentional in the ways you care for yourself.

Spending too much time alone is not helpful. You are in a very fragile state. Your thinking is likely to become more disordered, and you are more at risk of intrusive imagery and harmful memories, feeling numb and spaced out, or losing hope. Ask someone to come over and watch television with you, share a meal, or take a walk at a nearby park or lake. The human contact will be helpful.

Take care of your health. Drink lots of water, eat healthy meals, and exercise if you can, even if you're only walking around the block or taking a video yoga class in the privacy of your home. Physical symptoms are common after trauma, like digestive problems, headaches, back pain, weight loss or gain, or insomnia. Talk with a doctor if these are adding to the difficulties you are confronting.

Also, stay away from alcohol, opioids, marijuana, or other substances. It might seem like they can take the edge off or offer some relief from pain. Over time, however, they can more than boomerang, and you will end up in significantly worse shape. If you need to seek treatment for substance abuse, now is a good time to do that.

Be very careful what you put in writing, especially on social media, and ask friends and family to be mindful of this as well. Your attorney will tell you that there may be legal implications. It is probably best to stay off social media, and use email and texting sparingly. The throes of trauma can cause us to say and do things that can be misconstrued and distorted, causing further harm to ourselves or others.

Finally, and most importantly, be gentle with yourself. Try to support yourself with compassion and kindness as you face what's ahead. You've had a huge shock. You are in the midst of one of the most stressful situations you will ever experience. You face a mountain of consequences: psychological and spiritual, and possibly legal, financial, interpersonal, or health related. Your physical, mental, emotional, and spiritual stability likely will be profoundly challenged.

A helpful exercise is to imagine that your good friend is going through what you're enduring. Think about how you would talk to and treat that friend. Now do the same with yourself.

Treating ourselves kindly is more than difficult, as we will encounter again and again what we call the "Fallacy of the Three Ps."

The Fallacy of The Three Ps

In the immediate aftermath of your incident, you will be tempted to buy into The Fallacy of the Three Ps: personalization, pervasiveness, and permanence. These serve as unwanted harbors for feelings of debilitating guilt, shame, and sadness. Let's unpack them.

One of the phenomena we see quite often in unintentional harm is the severity and speed in which we can blame ourselves—for everything. We personalize it.

Sure, we may be at fault for the incident and may be to blame to some degree or another. But our tendency to take on more than our fair share of blame is typical. We think, "I should have taken a different route," "I should have had a friend drive me home," "I should never have owned a firearm in the first place.' Even if something was totally outside our control, we find ways to blame ourselves.

After all, most of us, by nature, are compassionate and understanding, especially for those in pain. When tragedy strikes, we ask, "How could I have prevented it?" Our brains are wired to find ways to build some kind of link between our capacities, real or imagined, to prevent unfortunate events. These thoughts may or may not be valid, but our tendency to universally blame ourselves and to personalize responsibility is common.

In the early stage of trauma, we are also very likely to perceive tragedy as pervasive in scope. We can feel that since we unintentionally harmed someone, every aspect of our lives is ruined; nothing is right. This feeling of comprehensive failure spreads to every aspect of our lives: our reputation is tarnished, our career is ruined, our family lives are destroyed. We cannot be a good parent, partner, neighbor, employee, sister, or uncle because we have caused unintentional harm. We walk around thinking that every person we meet knows every detail of what we have done and is viewing us accordingly. Our trauma puts an unhelpful lens of pervasiveness before us that makes us unable to separate any aspect of our lives from our trauma.

Finally, this initial stage of trauma tells us that the degree of pain we are feeling right now will never go away: it's permanent. Over and over, we may think that things will never get better. Since we have committed such an egregious act, it will hang over our heads, with all its weight, emotion, and precedence, for the rest of our lives—and beyond. We think we deserve this pain as penance. In this initial trauma stage, we have a hard time seeing past the pain of what we've done, telling ourselves that we had better get used to this hurt because it will never, ever decrease or go away.

But mental pain is a lot like physical pain: the hurt does let up, though the scar will always be there. And while these feelings of permanence, pervasiveness, and personalization, are real, they are also false.

There is hope.

Three Lessons

The early stages of trauma have profound effects on the brain and the rest of our bodies. Our trauma responses largely bypass our conscious control. Exercising willpower or wishing them away rarely works.

We have personally witnessed hundreds of Fellowship members go through the shock and trauma of those first few weeks, and from their experiences—and our own—we have learned three important lessons that can be help as you navigate these early stages.

First, in the vast majority of instances, it gets better.

Of course, it may not feel like it. You may be afraid that your life is ruined. You may be convinced that you will never "recover" from

---

this trauma, and perhaps you feel like you don't deserve to recover. You might be in such despair that you are thinking about suicide. But, hold on; be patient. We promise that, in all likelihood, you will not feel this hopeless anguish forever.

This is not to say that you can simply move on and leave the incident and all of its emotions behind you, like a storm that passes. Many cases of unintentional death take years to resolve. We need time to heal. We have to learn to manage our troubling thoughts, images, feelings, memories, and bodily sensations. We have to adjust to the frightening realization that we have less control over ourselves and our world than we used to believe. And we have to deal with the practical repercussions of these accidents, such as legal, financial, health-related, social, and occupational effects.

Secondly, you will most likely find a way to cope with your tragedy.

Think of an amputated limb. Initial mobility is difficult and painful. But over time, prosthesis may be fitted, wheelchairs and vans can be secured, and a new normal develops that allows life to adapt to a new normalcy that is not centered around the incident. The majority of us find ways to pick up the pieces and lead a fulfilling life. This terrible event does not define us.

Finally, while we feel defeated and disabled, there are important things we can do. We still have choices, agency, some modicum of control. Of course, we didn't choose to kill or injure someone. We didn't choose to cause so much grief and pain to others. And we didn't choose to have an acute stress reaction.

We didn't choose this endless barrage of intrusive images, emotions that sweep over us or that sense of depersonalization or numbness, which sets in regardless of our efforts to avoid it.

But we can choose to respond with integrity and compassion for ourselves and others affected. We can choose to ask for help from a therapist, doctor, clergy, family member, or friend so that we make sound decisions and actively cope with our symptoms. We can set goals and begin to chart a path forward. While we're in the midst of shock and trauma, we might not be ready to travel the path. But we can hold the intention, and that, in itself, will be helpful.

You may feel like your life is out of control, and you are breaking down. We've learned that "breakdown" means different things to different people, but sometimes we need to fall apart before we can rebuild. And that's okay. In fact, allowing yourself to experience this dark night of the soul can, over the long run, facilitate healing and recovery.

We urge you to ask for help from a therapist or clergy member for the psychological issues and a friend or family member with practical issues. This doesn't make you weak or dependent. It's a choice that shows respect for yourself and others.

Key Takeaways

* In the early days after the accident, you likely are experiencing a host of emotions associated with the trauma. You need emotional support—from a partner or spouse, a friend, a clergy person, or a therapist. Seek out someone to help through the first days of the crisis.

* We also strongly suggest that you fill out "The Early Stages Planning Form" that follows at the end of this chapter. It will help you move through some important decisions and keep track of contacts and other details.

Discussion Questions

1. Maryann offers important advice in the early days after an accidental killing: Job number one is getting trauma under control. What steps can you take to gain some control of the situation?

2. Who are some of the people you can call on to help you in these first few days of acute trauma? Make a list of the people who might be able to help. Be aware that your needs might change as time passes.

3. In what ways have you bought into "The Fallacy of the Three Ps: personalization, pervasiveness, and permanence"? How can you address each of these fallacies?

4. What can you do today to care for yourself as you navigate through these early days?

Unintentional Harm: The Early Stages Planning Worksheet

Today's date:

Listed below are several topics you'll want to start thinking about and planning for.

As you go through them, write tasks, noting what you need to get done right now or in the near term. Include deadlines.

But before you tackle this, write a short list of people you think can help. You can assign them to tasks as you work through the list. You can also download this worksheet from the Fellowship's website at hyacinthfellowship.org/resources.

People who can help:

Reflect on these legal/regulatory issues:

- Obtain referral(s) to a lawyer/schedule appointment.

- Who do you need to call for this?
  When are you able to schedule an appointment?

- Contact and/or follow up with law enforcement.

- List the agency/agencies involved including names and contact information.

- Contact and/or follow up with insurance company.

- List any insurance agencies involved including names and contact information.

- Other:

Reflect on these employment or education issues:

- Who do you need to call at work or school?
  List your employment or education contacts here, including names and contact information.

- What will you tell your boss, co-workers, peers, or teachers? When will you tell them?
  Work through how you want to communicate what has happened.
  List any additional employment or education stakeholders, including names and contact information.

■ Determine if you need time off, a modified schedule, or a modified work assignment.

■ Other:

Reflect on these health-related issues:

■ How will you obtain referral(s) to a psychotherapist and/or schedule appointments?
Who will you call? List names and contact information.

■ Do you need medical referral(s) for pain or injury/schedule appointment?
Who will you call? List names and contact information.

■ Do you need a referral to a psychiatrist for assessment for medication/schedule appointment?
Who will you call? List names and contact information.

■ What else is needed to take care of your health?

Reflect on these logistics of daily life

■ Do you need help with meals (even if it's just someone with whom to share the meal)? List names and contact information.

■ Do you need company? Can someone stay with you at important times, even just for a night or two?
List names and contact information.

■ What arrangements must be made for childcare? How can your children maintain their routines and activities?

■ What arrangements must be made for elder care? How can your elders maintain their routines and activities and get to appointments?

■ If you do not have access to a car or cannot drive, how will you handle transportation?

■ Are you able to run errands on your own? If not, who can do this for you or accompany you?

■ Now take a look at your planner. What plans, meetings, or appointments do you want/need to change or cancel?

■ Other:

Reflect on these family-related issues:

■ What do close relatives (e.g., spouse, partner, parents, siblings) need so they can support you most effectively?

■ What relatives should be informed, and how do you want to go about this?

■ What do your children or grandchildren know? What should they know? Who can they talk with about their feelings and concerns? What is needed so they can feel safe?

■ Are any family members traumatized, and, if so, how can they access counseling and support?

■ Other:

Reflect on these friends and community issues:

■ Who should be directly informed about this accident? List neighbors, close friends, and acquaintances. How do you want to go about this?

■ How do you want to manage your involvement in a religious congregation? Do you want to meet with the pastor, rabbi, or other clergy? Who will it be, where, and when?

■ What other community groups (e.g. book clubs, bike clubs, PTA, neighborhood associations, etc.) need to know about this, and what will you say?

■ Other:

Reflect on these media-related issues:

■ If you are getting media attention, how do you want to respond if at all? Who can advise you?

■ Should you shut down or restrict your presence on social media?

■ If you are being trolled or bullied online, how do you want to respond, if at all? Who can advise you?

■ Other:

CHAPTER THREE

The Anatomy of an Unintentional Killing: The Latter Stages of Pain

I live in the UK and was involved in a nighttime hunting accident in 2004 in which a 14-year-old boy was killed. I seemed to cope with it for eight years, but the thoughts and feelings have come back so strongly that life is now an everyday struggle. I think about his mum and family and feel such shame, remorse, and guilt. I didn't pull the trigger, but I made decisions that night that contributed significantly toward his death. I look at my own little girl and imagine how innocent he was, and it breaks my heart. I daily feel like ending it all. God, please help me. I am truly sorry for my sins. —Nick

If only the trauma of unintentional harm had some sort of expiration date...an on/off switch...or a magic potion that could slowly but surely erase the pain. But the reality is that, for most of us, as evidenced by Nick's story, our pain lingers for a long time, sometimes forever.

Once the initial trauma of our incidents begins to fade, we enter the latter stages of our pain. This is bittersweet. Yes, we've made it this far. We've learned how to cope, however imperfectly, but, as we learn from Nick's story, this does not mean we are healed, no longer suffering, or immune to what the future may bring.

It's important to know that our reactions to our incidents will likely evolve and that the scope of suffering is different for everyone. Some symptoms will fade, while new concerns might emerge. You will likely feel better in many ways, yet you will probably still have your difficult moments. This recurrent distress can be like a case of arthritis that never goes away and occasionally flares, sometimes very seriously.

In the latter stages of our trauma, several topics that command our attention include:

- Finding a long-term rhythm of healthy coping

- Envisioning a healthy post-incident life

- Thinking through a victim contact strategy

- Paying our debt to society/the victim

- Making peace with ourselves/others over what we have done

- Finding suitable answers to the "Why?" questions

While the journey is different for each person, we have found that many Fellowship members face distinctive challenges. These can be serious afflictions that often require professional help and significant investment to adequately address. There may be legal consequences to our actions. We may face social stigma, like bullying and retaliation. All this can lead to post-traumatic stress disorder, moral injury, and a host of related injuries endemic to those who have caused unintentional death or injury.

Post-traumatic Stress Disorder

I caused the death of my best friend when I was 15 years old. I'm nearly 40 now. He was a passenger on my motorcycle and sustained a catastrophic head injury when I crashed. The image burned into my brain is vivid and gruesome. For 25 years, I tried to cope with it on my own and in my own way. Everyone told me, "It's not your fault," and I thought that was enough. I can't stand hearing that now. I have severe but undiagnosed PTSD.

It has ruined every job and relationship I have ever had. The regret and intrusive thoughts are constant. I just lost a great, loving girl after a six-year relationship because of my short temper and antisocial behavior. She was the only girl I've ever loved. It was just too much for her, and I get it. It is absolutely gut-wrenching beyond explanation.

I can't hold down a job because of insomnia. I have the same horrible dreams that make me afraid to sleep. I'm trying to find help, but it's not easy for nonmilitary sufferers of PTSD, particularly because it's been so long since the accident. I will find my way, but to anyone who is reading this, please get help right away, even if you think you are fine. The sooner the better. These things creep in years later and can ruin your life if you ignore them, but they absolutely don't have to. I wish you all the best from the bottom of my heart. —Thom

Post-traumatic stress disorder, or PTSD, can be diagnosed when acute stress reactions last longer than 30 days. This is a very common experience among those who have unintentionally harmed as well as others who have been through a serious trauma.

These are some of the symptoms of PTSD. They fall into four categories.

- *Intrusion symptoms* refer to how images or memories of the event affect your waking and sleeping hours.

- *Avoidance symptoms* refer to how we try to skirt distressing feelings or stay away from external reminders of the trauma.

- *Negative alterations in cognition and mood* refer to difficulty remembering aspects of the incident; negative beliefs about ourselves or the world that we started feeling after the incident; negative emotions such as fear, guilt, and horror; feeling separate or detached from others; or being unable to feel positive emotions like happiness.

- *Arousal symptoms* include an exaggerated startle reaction, hypervigilance, difficulty concentrating, difficulty with sleep, angry outbursts, or reckless and self-destructive behavior.

It is not necessary to have all these symptoms to be diagnosed with PTSD. However, if the symptoms you display cause significant distress or impairment, a PTSD diagnosis may follow.

Generally, PTSD follows the traumatic incident closely in time, but sometimes the traumatic reaction occurs or recurs months or even years later. This is called delayed-onset PTSD. The treatments for PTSD are similar regardless of when it occurs.

Do You Suffer from Post-traumatic Stress Disorder (PTSD)?

The American Psychiatric Association describes the symptoms of PTSD, including the:

I. **Presence of one or more of the following intrusion symptoms, beginning after the traumatic event occurred:**

   A. Recurrent, involuntary, and intrusive distressing memories of the traumatic event

   B. Recurrent distressing dreams related to the traumatic event

   C. Dissociative reactions, such as flashbacks, in which the individual feels or acts as if the traumatic event was recurring

   D. Intense or prolonged psychological distress at exposure to internal or external cues that symbolize or resemble an aspect of the traumatic event

   E. Marked physiological reactions to internal or external cues that symbolize or resemble an aspect of the traumatic event

II. **Persistent avoidance of stimuli associated with the traumatic event**

   A. Avoidance of or efforts to avoid distressing memories, thoughts, or feelings about the traumatic event

B. Avoidance of or efforts to avoid external reminders (people, places, conversations, activities, objects, situations) that arouse distressing memories, thoughts, or feelings about the traumatic event

III. Negative alterations in cognitions and mood associated with the traumatic event

A. Inability to remember an important aspect of the traumatic event

B. Persistent and exaggerated negative beliefs or expectations about oneself, others, or the world (e.g., "I am bad," "No one can be trusted," "The world is completely dangerous," "My whole nervous system is permanently ruined")

C. Persistent, distorted cognitions about the cause or consequences of the traumatic event that lead the individual to blame himself/herself or others

D. Persistent negative emotional state (e.g., fear, horror, anger, guilt, or shame)

E. Markedly diminished interest or participation in significant activities

F. Feelings of detachment or estrangement from others

G. Persistent inability to experience positive emotions (e.g., inability to experience happiness, satisfaction, or loving feelings)

IV. **Marked alterations in arousal and reactivities associated with the traumatic event, beginning or worsening after the event occurred**

   A. Irritable behavior and angry outbursts (with little or no provocation) typically expressed as verbal or physical aggression toward people or objects

   B. Reckless or self-destructive behavior

   C. Hypervigilance

   D. Exaggerated startle response

   E. Problems with concentration

   F. Sleep disturbances (e.g., difficulty falling asleep or staying asleep or restless sleep)

Not all people who unintentionally harm develop PTSD and among those who do, the severity and duration will differ. It's important to remember that, like all diseases, mental or otherwise, the sufferer is not at fault: PTSD is not an indication of weakness or deficiency. It is a natural reaction our bodies take to cope with the events we've experienced.

The likelihood of developing PTSD depends on many different factors. The nature of your trauma is one. For instance, if the victim was a child, if you had a close-up view of the death or injury, or if there were multiple victims, you may be more likely to develop PTSD. Another factor in the development of PTSD is whether you've experienced trauma in the past. Your innate temperament and the way your nervous system functions are other factors.

The short-term response to the trauma also makes a difference, especially whether you receive strong support from others. Many Fellowship members face stress from legal processes, media coverage, or reverberations at home, work, or in the community; all of this can increase the likelihood of PTSD.

The Hyacinth Fellowship website has dozens of comments that describe what it's like to have PTSD.

PTSD is like a 300-pound backpack. I have learned to carry it, to ask for help, to rest, to give myself space. —Jim

I just feel unmotivated all the time now, and all I want to do is sleep. I used to be so happy and full of motivation to achieve my dreams, but I just feel like I am slowly losing myself. I've been doing badly in school and have been losing connections with friends who I used to be so close with. —Jose

[The accident] replays in my head 8-12 times a day. I feel selfish for getting help or talking about my pains. I'm 19, I'm broken, and I'm scared. —Kathryn

The feeling that the world might just be a place of uncontrolled chaos still lingers. I have not let the fear stop me from living, but I think about the accident daily, and I cannot shake the feeling that anything can happen at any time. —Cate

I work from home, and I have not been able to leave the house at all. I'm too scared to drive by where it happened, even from the passenger seat. I have no clue how to function normally...On the outside, I seem better, but on the inside, I replay the moment over and over and am finding it impossible to sleep. —Keisha

---

If you suspect you might have PTSD, you can find lots of self-assessments online, but only a psychotherapist or doctor is qualified to diagnose this. We've found that one of the better self-assessments is available from the Anxiety and Depression Association of America (ADAA); you can find it online on the ADAA website by searching for Screening for Post-traumatic Stress Disorder (PTSD). We recommend that you fill and print it out and bring it with you when you see a doctor or therapist.

We could easily spend the rest of this book (and more!) reviewing the science about how trauma affects our bodies and our brains. If you want that level of detail, we've listed some helpful books in the Resource section at the end of this book. For now, we want you to recognize that trauma affects our entire being: our conscious thoughts, our unconscious, our feelings and moods, our critical thinking and problem-solving abilities, our physical well-being, our sleep, and the way our brains and nervous systems react to different stimuli. Trauma and PTSD can be all-encompassing and interfere with our ability to function day-to-day, such as in parenting, working, taking care of a household, being a good spouse or friend, and so forth.

There is strong evidence that psychotherapy is helpful for treating PTSD. It can go away on its own, but working with a therapist can make this process less painful, less burdensome for others in your life (friends and family), and more efficient. Medication prescribed by a doctor can also be helpful, ideally in combination with psychotherapy. Self-help exercises can be useful in managing PTSD and are great adjuncts to therapy. If you feel stuck or hopeless, your day-to-day functioning is impaired, or you are experiencing disruptive symptoms such as flashbacks or depersonalization, a therapy appointment is in order.

Post-traumatic stress is emotional, cognitive, spiritual, and physical in its effects and symptoms. Traditional talk therapy can be effective in treating PTSD. In addition, many therapists are turning to methods that bypass the "rational" mind and work on other levels. Chapter 6 describes some options for treatment.

Dealing with post-traumatic stress (in therapy or on one's own) can not only reduce problematic symptoms but also lead to increased insight, compassion, and inner strength. Psychologists call this post-traumatic growth. Through personal and spiritual growth, we are better able to live meaningful lives and help others. We believe this is a worthy goal.

A note about depression: Depressive disorders often co-occur with PTSD. If you have persistent feelings of sadness or low mood, inability to feel pleasure, and changes in your patterns of sleeping or eating, a doctor or psychotherapist may recommend treatment for depression. There are areas of overlap and differences between recommended treatments for PTSD and depression, and both may be helpful. In general, we find that finding the right diagnosis is less important than finding the right therapist who understands this complexity.

Moral Injury

I hate myself every day for taking [the victim] away from his family and friends and for putting other lives in danger on the roadway. He is behind every thought I have. The moment I find myself happy, I can't help but make it stop because I know he can't enjoy life, and it's my fault, so why should I? —Kelly

The survivor guilt is real. I've been single pretty much my whole life, and I think it's because I don't feel like I deserve to be loved. —Sarah

If I had paid more attention, been more firm, hadn't been so burnt out, I could have saved [the patient], but I didn't. I don't know how I can live with myself, when I was supposed to be helping people, not hurting them. This happened in my early 20s, and I am still haunted by it. I feel like I can never be happy again and that I must suffer for what I've done. —Madeline

There are the nightmares, the guilt, the engulfing sadness, the realization that even though it was an accident, I caused a life to end. How do I live with that? How dare I drink wine or feel the sun on my face when she cannot? —Alex

---

As we see from these Fellowship members, while we may have escaped our incidents without physical pain, chances are that we've suffered a particular hurt on the inside. We may have developed a moral injury.

By definition, moral injury is the result of falling short of our moral standards or violating our "core moral beliefs," as described in the book, *Soul Repair: Recovering from Moral Injury after War* by Gabriella Lettini and Rita Nakashima Brock. Think of someone who has been brought up to believe killing is wrong, then becomes a soldier whose job is to kill, or a nurse who pledged an oath to heal and cure, then unintentionally gives a patient the wrong medication that causes death. Most everyone lives by or espouses some version of the Golden Rule: "Do unto others what you would like done unto you." Killing someone, even unintentionally, violates that fundamental moral tenet, one that applies across cultures, nations, and religions. And this violation of our moral code—our consciences—can cause devastating harm.

Brock explains: "Moral injury is intensely painful. It's a deep kind of suffering because you feel like in a high-stakes situation, something went wrong and you couldn't prevent it, or you actually did what caused the harm. Those intensely painful feelings are a sign that the good part of you wants to come back. But it won't come back if you keep pushing those feelings down, not paying attention to them."

While PTSD is primarily fear-based, moral injury is rooted in guilt and shame. Guilt, of course, is the feeling we get when we've done something wrong, when we regret our behavior, impulses, or thoughts and feelings. Shame is about who we are, not just what we've done. Shame tells us that not only did we do a bad thing but also that we are bad people. When we're ashamed, we feel exposed and inadequate.

Where guilt can motivate us to take action and make amends, shame makes us want to run away and hide. Shame is more difficult to manage than guilt because of its all-encompassing nature, but both extreme guilt and shame can leave us stuck in misery.

The concept of moral injury emerged from work with soldiers and veterans. Even when they received treatment for PTSD, these soldiers and veterans remained distressed. The PTSD treatment did not address the moral component of military service such as killing in combat or perhaps harming civilians or mistakes such as friendly fire. What clergy and psychologists discovered was that the soldiers who violated their own moral standards suffered long-term consequences.

In order to heal, the veterans and soldiers had to both acknowledge the moral transgression(s) and restore a sense of themselves as deserving and capable of goodness.

Unlike PTSD, moral injury is still a new concept. It's not in the Diagnostic and Statistical Manual of Mental Disorders, the bible of psychiatric diagnoses that therapists use, and there is less research and writing about it. That situation is changing, however, and every month, new articles appear in academic journals. Although most of the research still focuses on the military, moral injury has been studied among healthcare providers, educators, law enforcement, child protection workers, and, most recently, those who have unintentionally harmed.

Signs of moral injury include guilt, shame, hopelessness, depression, remorse, re-experiencing, withdrawal, and social isolation. Addiction and suicidal ideation may also be outcomes of moral injury, as well as spiritual questioning or a loss of faith. Studies generally identify three categories of moral injury symptoms:

■ Self-injury, including suicidal feelings and substance abuse. Moral injury can make us feel like life is not worth living. It can lead us to dull the pain with alcohol, drugs, or other addictions like sex or food.

■ Demoralization, which means feeling worthless, being mired in despair, and feeling like your life, or life in general, has no meaning and offers no fulfillment. If you have a moral injury, you may believe that, since you no longer consider yourself a good person, your life has no meaning or value. You might feel sad or apathetic much of the time. Activities you used to enjoy may no longer engage your interest.

■ Self-handicapping. You may not allow yourself to feel any positive emotions, telling yourself that you don't deserve happiness or pleasure. Any time you start to feel good, you shut down. You may also isolate yourself and avoid other people, even (or especially) those who love you and want to support you. And you might reject the idea of therapy or counseling because you don't feel deserving of comfort.

You might notice that these symptoms overlap with PTSD. Many Fellowship members have both.

If you suspect you might be suffering from moral injury, take the Moral Injury and Distress Scale assessment available on the U.S. Department of Veterans website. It will give you a good sense of the extent to which moral injury is affecting your day-to-day life.

A Spiritual Injury

Moral injury can also be considered a spiritual malady—a wound to the soul. Given this perspective, it is not surprising that many clergy encounter people who have moral injury.

All the major religious traditions hold a high view of humanity that is not based on what we do but on who we are. We are deemed worthy of life and entrusted with huge responsibilities not because we're being tested or harshly judged but because we are purposefully created, inherently loved, and given the gift of channeling that love into the world. Humans make mistakes. We get caught up in all sorts of harmful situations that may or may not be our fault. When our ethical codes are violated, most of which are rooted in our spiritual convictions of authority and morality, we can see ourselves as hopelessly condemned or damned by these actions. Finding ways to align these beliefs with our innate self-worth and purpose becomes the difficult but needful work we have ahead of us.

Where we have seen promising progress in treating moral injury is when the aim is not to eliminate guilt but to address it. Instead of "moral reassurance," the emphasis is on "moral repair," according to psychologist Matt J. Gray. Despite our incident and its terrible consequences, self-forgiveness is possible and allows us to move forward with compassion, virtue, and caring.

We have found that moral injury heals most effectively when we allow ourselves to accept support from others and just as importantly, when we contribute to the community. This includes participating in shared activities, supporting or serving others, and helping to create safer and more caring communities.

This means fighting the tendency to withdraw from others. Allowing yourself to be in community and in relationship with others can be scary. You might experience new waves of guilt crashing over you at the idea that you don't have to punish yourself for the rest of your life. It takes strength to heal from moral injury, just as it does from trauma, but we know that most people can find that strength inside and outside of them.

Although some people can heal from moral injury on their own, most need help. When we are in the grip of this injury, we tend to avoid our feelings because they are so painful. When we acknowledge that we failed to live up to our moral standards, we conclude that our self-contempt and self-punishment are deserved. We end up in an uncomfortable pattern of withdrawal from ourselves and others, self-punishment, and self-denigration. We deny ourselves pleasure, pride, or self-respect. If this sounds like you, reach out for help. We talk more about unintentional harm and spirituality in Chapter 5.

Related Injuries

While some of us may have avoided PTSD and serious bouts with moral injury, most of us still struggle. Our incidents have permanently affected our beliefs about ourselves and our beliefs about our world. We have been injured in serious ways that need our attention. You may be able to relate to some or all of these.

Loss of Trust in Ourselves and Our World

The feeling that the world might just be a place of uncontrolled chaos still lingers. I have not let the fear stop me from living, but I think about the accident daily, and I cannot ever shake the feeling that anything can happen at any time. —Charlotte

We know firsthand that terrible things can happen in a split second. As a result, our newfound awareness may make us more vigilant and anxious. After Maryann's car crash, driving became so difficult that she gave up her car for almost two years, but her fear carried over to all kinds of settings. Wherever children gathered, she saw the potential for harm. Instead of enjoying the excitement of little kids playing at the beach, for instance, she watched to make sure they were safe from drowning. This type of response is not uncommon.

For many of us, the world suddenly seems full of danger and risk. Of course, we knew long before our incidents that unintentional harm and other tragedies occur, but we were good at keeping that awareness at a distance. It was useful to believe that the world is a safe place, even though, on some level, we knew better. But now that we have unintentionally harmed, this illusion of safety is shattered. No place is safe. The world seems capricious, unpredictable, and even cruel.

On top of no longer trusting the world, we may lose trust in ourselves. Before our incidents, we probably felt competent and confident of our abilities (e.g., driving, owning a gun, caring for a child, or managing a household). But afterward, many of us fear that we are not nearly as competent as we thought. Our vitality, once a source of pride and happiness, now scares us. What if we harm someone else?

Self-Punishment and Denial of Happiness

Every time something good happens, I remind myself that I killed someone. His children are growing up without a father. I won't let myself feel good. —Sun

We live in a contractual world: we do something, and we get paid accordingly. So, what happens when we do something so heinous as to take a life? We believe we should get paid accordingly.

So, we pay ourselves back by punishing ourselves. We deny ourselves pleasurable activities, we isolate ourselves, and let others treat us badly or even abuse us. We physically harm ourselves, abuse substances, and constantly tell ourselves how bad and unworthy we are. We don't allow others to love us, much less allow for self-love.

Maybe we hope that if we suffer enough, we will eventually find redemption. We think that if we show ourselves, the world, and God how awful we feel, we can find forgiveness and acceptance.

But this reasoning quickly falls short. Self-harm will not bring a dead person back to life, it will not change the circumstances that caused our incident, and it will not do us much good as we undertake the work of healing ourselves or others.

Our way forward must be marked by truth-telling, forgiveness, apology, and a resolve to live not simply for ourselves but for the memory of those we have harmed. We do ourselves or others no good by wallowing in despair and self-flagellation. We may deserve to be punished, but this delicate issue must be faced with practicality and compassion.

Relationship Problems

My accident was more than twenty years ago. My wife and I were newly married at the time, and our way of dealing with it was to just push through it. We dealt with the legal proceedings head-on, then we went on about life. Now, twenty-four years later, there are issues going on that my therapist believes tie directly to the fact that we never truly dealt with the emotional impact of my accident. —Darcy

Today, I got a call from my husband. He was crying more than I've ever heard. He said someone ran out in front of his big work truck, and the person was killed instantly. My husband and I have been together since we were 15, and we are 31 now. I always make everything better, and it's killing me that I can't take his pain away. I don't know what to do for him. I want to be there for him. I don't want to hover, but I also don't want to leave him alone with his thoughts. I'm just lost. —Sparrow

I'm getting married in June, and I haven't even spoken to him about it. I'm sure it will come out when we live together because when I have a "flashback," I make a noise and start crying. I am just so used to not talking about it that I don't know how to tell him. —Nina

---

We hear statements like this over and over again. Our incidents have caused rifts and ripples in our close relationships. For many of us, our friends and family members love us, but they don't understand us. They don't understand how to help, why we can't let go of self-blame and guilt, or why we don't feel like going out or being around other people. They don't understand why we continue to be so upset when it was "just an accident."

They may also be anxious and worried. Will their loved one go to jail? Will the family face a lawsuit? Are friends and neighbors judging the situation? This anxiety can make it more difficult for our loved ones to listen, and they may rush in to try to "fix" the situation.

Furthermore, the shame and guilt of our injury make many of us feel like hiding from the world. We want to crawl into a cave and stay there, away from the scrutiny of others. We may push others away and refuse to engage or share our thoughts and feelings. And, when we do come out of our caves, we have limited ability to listen and empathize with others. Compared to what we did, other problems may seem trivial. And, we may not have the attention and bandwidth to offer support, especially if we are constantly being hijacked by intrusive images, memories of our incidents, and emotional distress.

We may also hold back from expressing our thoughts and feelings because we don't want to distress those who love us. Our spouse, parents, co-workers, or friends might be doing extra duty like taking on more responsibility at home or at work. We know they are worried about us, and we fear that if we share what's going on inside, they will be even more worried. So, we keep everything bottled up inside and try to soldier on.

All of this takes a toll on family relationships and friendships. We often long to connect and support one another, but we miss the boat. And we feel so sad.

There is no magic fix for this, especially if the relationship was troubled before the incident. Our advice is to try to express appreciation to family and friends for their love and concern, even if it falls short in some ways. Try to guide them in how to support you. Let them know what you need, keeping in mind what they are capable of providing. Some can give you practical help (you need a ride to a lawyer's office, for instance). Some can give you companionship (let's eat a bowl of popcorn and stream a movie). And some can offer emotional support and listen or hold us (physically or metaphorically) while we cry.

An important caveat: if you think you need to be alone all the time and find yourself telling friends and family, without exception, to leave you alone or back off, you are probably in the tight grip of trauma or moral injury. Give yourself a balance of alone time and time with others. That can include time with a therapist or counselor. Isolation may feel safe, but we have learned it will perpetuate despair.

Litigation and Prosecution

Even though I was found not guilty in a criminal jury trial, it took all my savings for lawyers and therapists and consultants to hold myself together and to defend myself. Then there was the civil trial with pre-trial mediations full of screaming accusations and so much grief and anger. They were furious that I had not been found guilty. Psychologically, I became walled-off and single-focused. I had been an outgoing and gregarious person all of my life, but I became depressed and anxious; sleep was non-existent, and joy was out of reach. I eventually had to declare bankruptcy. The victim's family never got any money because I didn't have any.

My grief for the family is still active. I forgive them. But it is still very hard for me to forgive myself. It was hard to fight for a not-guilty verdict because I felt so guilty about the death of their child. I was suicidal for a while. I tried to have empathy. I'm not a saint, but I found it was too painful to hold the strong emotion of anger. —Lamont

Sometimes, trauma gets added to trauma. The moral and emotional injury that stems from the incident itself is one thing. When we are prosecuted, sued, or subject to other kinds of blame and retaliation, trauma is worsened.

A minority of Fellowship members will face criminal charges for misdemeanors and felonies. Many more will face lawsuits. We do not attempt to critique the criminal justice system here. We believe that healing involves accepting responsibility and accountability, especially for those of us who were negligent or reckless. We also recognize that the U.S. courts are imperfect, inconsistent, sometimes unjust and cruel, and at times simply wrong. At best, the outcome will be both just and merciful. But, many of us find the process to be long and painful and feel that the outcome is unfair. Of course, many of our victims feel the same way.

Involvement in the courts can be traumatic. It is difficult to heal from emotional pain, PTSD, moral injury, and the assorted ways our incidents have affected us in the face of this stress and uncertainty, especially since the consequences can be life-changing. As we've mentioned, it is essential to hire your own attorney and to work with a therapist. The miniscule risk that the courts will ask the therapist to violate confidentiality should not keep you from seeking professional support and help. Just as you put a legal team together to help defend and protect you, so too do you need a personal and emotional support team to guard and protect you. The literal trials and tribulations that may be ahead must be taken seriously and prepared for accordingly.

Bullying and Retaliation

Five years ago, I accidentally shot and killed my niece...Over the past five years, I have worked so hard to try and get my life together. I started a new job about a year ago and have been doing well for myself. Then yesterday happened. I knew it might become public some day, but someone at work Googled me and found my arrest and showed it to all the other employees. I'm having a hard time...I'm not even sure if I should go back to work. I feel ashamed, lost, guilty. It was like a ton of bricks. It feels like it just happened all over again. —Abe

In the months after the accident, I was very traumatized. Local newspapers villainized me for months. I refused to watch the news or read any newspapers. The trolls added

---

further trauma, which I will never fully recover from. People can say the cruelest things. They needed someone to blame, someone to hate. They chose me. —Shantai

Twenty-two years ago, when I was 20, I was the driver in a drunk driving accident that killed my best friend. Not only were we best friends, but also our families had been longtime friends. I became the town pariah. I immediately became "that guy," the villain in everyone's movie. On a few occasions, different people said to me, "Oh, you're the one who killed that boy." I eventually moved away and except for three times, I have never talked about it since. —Eric

I was punched in the face by the boy's brother, and his mother attacked me...I was in all the papers and on the news even though I was only 17 at the time. I went back to high school after my accident one week before graduation. I was taunted, hit, laughed at, picked on, had things thrown at me, was called a murderer, on and on. I graduated, and it was silent when I walked on stage. —Chet

Regardless of the legal processes and consequences, Fellowship members may face harsh criticism, bullying, and retaliation. Increasingly, this occurs online on social platforms and media comment sections. Friends of the victim may express their anger online, but often online "trolls" with no direct connection to the incident seem to take pleasure in shaming and hurting people. Becoming a victim of online bullying, harassment, or lies is hurtful and compounds trauma. You can take steps to address this problem, although there is no way to entirely eliminate it.

Online Bullying:
What Should You Do?

We have found it best not to respond to online critics, no matter how inflammatory their comments. Appeals to people's better nature, explanations, and arguments will not help and are likely to make the problem worse. Resist the temptation to respond, set the record straight, or even hit back. You may want to consider asking a friend to offer factual corrections only.

We recommend you keep copies of the harmful posts or comments, or, even better, entrust a friend with this unpleasant task. If the harassment escalates, you may need a record. If you have a lawyer, show the posts to them and ask for advice.

The major social media platforms have procedures and policies in place for dealing with defamation, harassment, trolling, and threats. Read and follow the recommendations for reporting violations of their policies. Also, follow the recommendations for protecting your privacy. Of course, the best way to protect your online privacy is to leave these platforms. You may want to consider suspending or terminating your accounts, at least for a while.

If the harassment crosses a line to threats to harm you or those close to you, report the offender to the platform but also contact local law enforcement. They can perform a threat assessment and take action, if needed.

Unfortunately, bullying and retaliation are not only restricted to the internet. Some of us have been harassed in other ways, such as taunts and name-calling, threatening telephone calls, damage to one's car or home, or threats of physical violence (or, rarely, actual violence). Such behavior should be reported to the authorities.

No matter what, you do not deserve to be publicly shamed, harassed, trolled, or threatened. Such behaviors are cruel, destructive, and may be illegal. Work with your support system to manage the fear, shame, anger, and hurt such behavior stimulates. Despite the old schoolyard rhyme, words can and do hurt us, but we can also recognize when they are untrue, intended to wound, and say more about the speaker than about you.

Handling the harm we experience as Fellowship members is where we turn next.

Key Takeaways

* After the initial incident, many people who have accidentally killed or seriously injured someone face distinctive challenges such as post-traumatic stress disorder and moral injury. We may experience social stigmas like bullying or retaliation, ongoing trauma from prosecution and litigation, and difficulty in forming and maintaining relationships. These can be serious challenges that often require professional help and significant investment to adequately address. But there is hope— and help.

Discussion Questions

1. Have you ever considered that you might suffer from PTSD? Have you taken an assessment? If not, why? What's stopping you?

2. Have you heard about the concept of moral injury before? How does the description resonate in your life? What steps are you taking toward healing of that injury?

3. How has your incident affected your relationships? With a spouse or partner? Child/ren? Parents? Friends? Co-workers? Make an honest assessment, both on your own and in conversation with those people who care about you. How might you seek to strengthen those relationships?

CHAPTER FOUR

The Emotional Toll of Unintentional Harm

A witness told police there was nothing I could have done. Moments before, another car had run out of gas and pulled to the side of the road, and the passenger had gotten out of the car. A deer ran in front of my car, my car hit their car, and their car hit the man. When police arrived, the man wasn't alive. I did go to therapy, but it's just such a different thing, and there is nobody I know who has been through this. I know rationally it wasn't my fault, but I have this heavy heart and guilt about surviving. I wonder why I survived, and he didn't. I wonder if I should be doing something extraordinary because I'm alive and so easily could have lost my own life. I think about him every day. —Jake

The state attorney ruled it an accident, but I am not so easily convinced. I did go to therapy for four months after the accident, and the therapist has been incredible and literally kept me alive. At least suicide is no longer a viable option— and it was for months. I don't ever want to forget, but I need to get back to living. I have not even told my brothers about the accident for fear of being judged and shamed, and for once, I am glad my parents are deceased because they would be crushed. Obviously, I can judge and shame myself on my own. Every day, I think of the family left behind and pray for them to find some peace. I don't expect them to forgive me. I think about them on holidays without their dad, husband, and grandpa. I think about them during hurricanes, major news events, and when I accidentally laugh out loud or find myself enjoying a meal. —Janeanne

Will I ever get over this guilt? I'm exhausted from crying, and I feel sick to my stomach every day. Everything is a constant reminder of the accident, and it has consumed my every thought. I have only told my immediate family, colleagues, and one close friend, but I downplay everything because I am so ashamed and embarrassed. —Mark

---

Long after we've learned to cope with any physical injuries caused by our event, the emotional toll lingers. Indeed, for those who unintentionally harm, our feelings of guilt, shame, embarrassment, and responsibility damage us the most.

Guilt is the dominant and most long-lasting reaction for many of us. Even as our shock and grief wane, guilt still pierces us. What we did was unintentional, but our actions caused serious injury or death. That's a big deal.

Under most circumstances, guilt is motivating. It signals us to take action, make amends, or fix a problem. But extreme guilt can become paralyzing and interfere with our ability to work, parent, relate to others, or feel positive emotions.

The challenge is not to rid ourselves of our emotional reactions but to manage them so we are not controlled by them. We need to acknowledge these feelings as a sign of our humanity and caring—and then channel that energy in constructive directions.

When Authorities Exonerate You

I sent everything I could afford to the funeral home. His family reached out, and I spoke with them. There are no hard feelings or blame, but I can't stop blaming myself. The accident replays in my head a dozen times a day. I feel selfish for getting help or talking about my pain. I'm 19. I'm broken, and I'm scared. —Martha

I have absolutely no memory of the minutes leading up to the accident, save one, and that's of the exact moment of impact when I realized what was about to happen. For me, being unable to recollect what caused such a tragedy is the hardest part. I have never remembered my dreams in the past, but now I have the most vivid and disturbing dreams. Where I was once very driven and had achieved quite a bit in my career, I have zero motivation. I don't even want to clean the house. I feel lost. Angry. Like a victim (?) because I know in my heart that I did nothing to consciously be negligent or reckless. I grieve for the other driver. I grieve for myself. I feel like the "old me" is dead. I don't know what to do or how to be. I'm just miserable. I even feel anger and resentment toward the other driver for being there at that time, which makes me feel awful. I wish I could be normal again and feel happy. It seems like I never will. —Wylie

---

Some who cause unintentional harm are not legally or civilly culpable or responsible for the fatality in which they were involved. For example, a bicyclist might run a stoplight and collide with a car; a drunk may wander onto a dark freeway and get hit; or a nurse might have no way of knowing that the patient is allergic to a prescribed medication. The same goes for someone who lacks control over their behavior. We don't blame someone who caused

---

a collision because they had a sudden heart attack. If you're in this category, most likely others do not hold you blameworthy or culpable either.

Although you may find some solace in the fact that you are not to blame and aren't dealing with criminal charges in court, you probably still feel traumatized, guilty, and ashamed. Our natural wiring as people created out of goodness to do goodness has been violated. So many Fellowship members tell us they blame themselves even if no one else blames them.

This guilt is painful, and many people don't understand its depths. They often try to minimize the significance of the accident or try to relieve you of your guilt by reminding you that you were not at fault. Even when it's nice to receive such reassurance, such comments can also make us feel alone, like no one understands what it's like and no one wants to hear about it. It seems like others are telling us to just get over it and move on, but sometimes we can't move on.

What's important to note about these kinds of comments is that they are not always made solely for our benefit. Humans don't like to be around people who are in pain. We find it uncomfortable so we try to alleviate and "fix" the distress of others. Often, the motivation behind the "just get over it" comments has as much to do with the discomfort of those who say such things as it does in assisting us in coping with our guilt.

So why do we feel guilty about fatalities or injuries that weren't our fault?

Blaming ourselves is one way to avoid the fright of helplessness. The idea that anything can happen at any time—that we lack control over our experience and our world—is terrifying. Psychologists say that our "illusion of control" is helpful and even essential to our effective functioning. When trauma and PTSD destroy that illusion, we feel vulnerable, helpless, and afraid. Our unconscious may decide that feeling guilty is preferable and so we move to self-blame.

Another reason we blame ourselves is that some of us don't believe in accidents. Maybe you've long told yourself that "everything happens for a reason." You reject the idea of chance or random events. If so, you might wonder if unintentionally harming someone is a punishment from God or a message from your unconscious or from the universe. Or perhaps you tell yourself that we create the conditions of our lives and manifest what we want or need. (This is a staple of "new age" thinking.) If so, did you "manifest" a fatality?

And there are more down-to-earth reasons we blame ourselves, too.

For instance, you might not remember aspects of your accident. While this is a common occurrence in response to traumatic events, it also means that you can't be 100% sure of what really happened and must rely on other people's accounts. You might wonder if another person would have responded better under the circumstances and somehow avoided the accident.

Our emotional reaction to our events is a very human response to involvement in a fatal accident. What would we think about a person who didn't feel guilt, shame, or remorse? Some psychologists call our feelings "non-moral guilt" and consider them a sign of caring and connection to others, even though they are also a cause of anguish.

In our Fellowship meetings, we often talk about our emotional reactions as being significant signposts of our health and compassion. Many of us would change places with our victims if we could, go bankrupt if it could bring them back, and make all kinds of significant sacrifices if we could turn back the clock. These feelings and intentions are not to be ignored or diminished but to remind us that while we have done a bad thing, we are good people.

Instead of telling yourself that you "shouldn't" think or feel a certain way, allow yourself to explore your beliefs and feelings about the accident. If you are blaming yourself or holding onto irrational beliefs, consider why you are reluctant to give them up. Could these beliefs be a form of self-protection even though they are painful?

If you are dealing with some amnesia or uncertainty about what really occurred, it's useful to acknowledge that you may have to live with incomplete information. An accurate appraisal of your role in the incident can help you decide how you want to respond, without being harshly self-punishing or, at the other extreme, trying to act like it's no big deal.

When Authorities Find You at Fault

While I know it was an accident, I caused the accident. I was ticketed and couldn't get my license until I was 18. Her parents tried to have the state charge me with vehicular manslaughter, but they never brought charges against me because I was a minor and the victim was the adult in the car. I moved away as soon as I could, and I don't go back there often... I have been able to make a decent life for myself in a place where people don't know my past, but I still think about how people would feel about me if they knew the truth. I think I disassociated myself from my life for the years after the accident until I moved away. I try to make an effort to be present in my life now, but I struggle. —Skip

When I was 19 years old, under the influence of drugs and alcohol, I accidentally shot and killed my friend as we were playing with a gun... I was eventually sentenced to eight years in prison for manslaughter. His family and many of my close friends hated me afterward, rightfully so. I have hated myself ever since. I am 30 years old now. I live each day in a fog, and I am in constant pain. I have learned to live in isolation, avoiding people and crowded places. There is a deep pain inside that I don't know how to talk about, let alone explain. I have tried to self-medicate, tried to live sober, and have contemplated suicide. I seem to have ups and downs. But I have ultimately failed at being productive with relationships and jobs. —Peggy

If your negligence or error caused injury or death, the emotional toll will likely be greatly exacerbated.

In these cases, it's important to remember that being responsible for another person's death because of your own error or negligence does not mean that you did it on purpose or that you willed the result. It does not mean you are a bad person. It does not mean you are forever doomed to shame and guilt. It means you made a mistake. You cannot go back and undo that mistake, but you can decide how to respond now that it's happened.

Under these circumstances, feelings of guilt, embarrassment, and shame are reasonable, even natural. Regret and remorse are appropriate and important. But these feelings can become paralyzing, interfering with your day-to-day functioning and your ability to work, parent, or relate to others.

If you are reading this book, you probably do not need a lesson on accountability. Chances are you have accepted responsibility for the damage done. But a rigorous and honest appraisal of your responsibility is important to your healing. Were you distracted or impaired when the accident occurred? Did fatigue or anger contribute to bad decision-making? Were you trying something beyond your skill level? Recognizing what led to the incident is essential to avoiding the same mistake in the future. It also allows you to squarely confront "what is" so that you can deal with the feelings that emerge. Our efforts to avoid distress almost always end up perpetuating it.

For many of us, our incidents prompt us to conduct a serious personal inventory, to take a time-out so we can assess where we've been and where we're going. Perhaps this inventory can help us improve ourselves and even, in some way, honor our victims. An inventory may mean taking a serious look at issues.

- If you were under the influence of alcohol or drugs at the time of your accident, it is time to choose abstinence and seek treatment.

- If you were fatigued, it's time to examine why you were so tired and consider whether you need to make adjustments to your schedule or consult a doctor.

- If anger or rage clouded your judgment, it's time to look for an anger management group or talk with a therapist.

- If your skills weren't up to the task, it's time to get some additional training.

- If you acted negligently or selfishly, it's time to find ways to stop cutting corners and do the right thing, even if it is inconvenient, uncomfortable, or costly.

If you are considered blameworthy for the accident, you may be facing criminal or civil litigation. This can become confusing because, on the one hand, you recognize responsibility, and, on the other hand, you are trying to defend yourself. Victim's families can displace their feelings of loss with anger, vengeance, and painful outbursts that may well exceed the bounds of reasonable recourse. The legal and civil processes can be so drawn-out, acrimonious, and painful that you may feel victimized by the courts and lawyers, or you may believe that the consequences are unfair to you or your family. All this confusion speaks to the benefits of finding a good lawyer to be your advisor and advocate—and a good therapist.

We also note that involvement in legal proceedings adds to the trauma of the accident itself. There is so much that is out of your control, anxiety-provoking, upsetting, triggering, puzzling, and frustrating.

Endless self-punishment, skirting responsibility, or avoiding the truth serve no one. Acknowledging the truth, feeling your feelings, seeking support, and taking steps to honor your victim or make amends will let you regain your self-regard and help create kinder, more caring, and safer communities. You are so much more than your mistake.

Secrets, Disclosure, and Discretion

I've hidden the accident from my new boyfriend. Is this something I have to tell him? I feel incredible shame because of it, but I also feel like I'm keeping secrets from him. I don't know if he has a right to know or if I have a right to keep it to myself. —Carrie

I know that many people have experienced terrible tragedies in life. Being a nurse makes me even more acutely aware of that. I am a fairly open person with people I know well, but even after all these years, I've only told a couple of very trusted co-workers about my accident. It's the one thing that I just don't really talk about. Looking back at my life, I've always felt like the more time I place between when it happened and myself, the more "removed" I will be from it. It's hard to explain, but lately, I am realizing that this is just not true. —Phil

Amid the extra stress of the current atmosphere of the world, everything, including underlying stresses and triggers, feels closer to the surface—and more difficult to ignore. Even though the accident occurred more than five years ago, it is an active burden I cannot afford to carry any longer. I have a therapy appointment tomorrow, and I'm thinking about discussing the accident. I'm still absolutely terrified: will she judge me? Will I finally have to answer for it? Will talking about it actually help? The more I sit with my anxiety of merely talking about it, the more that all the old shame and terror of the consequences resurfaces. What consequences will come of mentioning it in therapy, aside from having to feel all those emotions? Will any good come of this? It feels like a terrible idea, but the other option—silence—hurts every bit as much. —Candace

In the immediate aftermath of your event, it may seem like everyone knows what you did. There might be media coverage, neighborhood gossip, or social media posts. The news spreads at work or at school. The anxiety and self-consciousness this engenders can add to distress. And it's much worse if those who identify with the victim ostracize, judge, criticize, spread false information, or seek retaliation.

Some Fellowship members have changed jobs, transferred schools, or moved to a different city to escape the stigma. Others find that, over time, this element of their identity becomes less visible. They acquire new neighbors or co-workers, other events displace their incident in the news, and the event fades into the past, at least for those not directly involved.

Many of us keep our accidents secret. This protects us from retaliation and judgment, but the impulse toward secrecy may have other elements. You might tell yourself that talking about it could make other people uncomfortable or bring back memories you'd rather keep stashed away. You don't want to appear weak or expose your shame or sadness. You don't want pity from others, and you don't believe you deserve support or sympathy.

There are at least two problems with the decision for secrecy.

Secrets create a gap between the way we present ourselves to others and the person we know ourselves to be. That gap puts distance between us and others. We cannot feel truly known and accepted or loved for who we are because we are not sharing who we are. This chronic emotional deprivation means we have less to give others. That is a sad and lonely way to live.

The second problem with secrets is that they allow irrational beliefs to take root. We get stuck in our own "narrative" about the accident —why it happened, what it means, and what we should do about it. Perhaps you have convinced yourself that you are a bad or dangerous person. Perhaps you believe that you will be hated and rejected if you share what happened. When we keep a secret, our shame tends to build up until it becomes a solid wall, keeping us from intimacy, joy, pride in ourselves, and a sense of community.

If this seems like your experience, it's time to look at how secrecy is serving you and how it is hurting you. Is your secret getting in the way of intimacy, community, or happiness? If so, maybe it's time to confide in someone. Honesty and vulnerability build intimacy. Intimacy helps us heal and adds meaning to our lives. So, who do we turn to?

We have found that the safest people to confide in are therapists and clergy, who are trained to deal with difficult disclosures and have a lot of experience hearing secrets. Over time, they can help you decide who you want to confide in, how, and why. You are likely to feel a great sense of relief—as if you've shed a heavy burden.

The opposite of secrecy is not necessarily full disclosure. This is where discretion comes into play. Presented with your story, some listeners will judge or pull away. Some will try to talk you out of your feelings or minimize what happened. There are plenty of ways that disclosure can go wrong.

We might also disclose because we harbor a wish deep inside us for someone else to take up or share our burdens. Be careful of this. It's mature and constructive to ask for support. It's unreasonable for adults to expect or ask someone to take charge of us.

Also, be careful of your choices if you tend to punish yourself. Have you picked a truly safe and kind person to confide in or have you picked someone who will have difficulty empathizing?

Again, discretion is vital. This means confiding in the people you trust, at a safe time and place. You might feel more emotional than expected. (It's okay to cry or feel super nervous.) And it's important to realize that your friend or relative may need time to process the information you share.

Part of discretion is also recognizing why you are choosing to confide and what outcome you want. For instance, you might say to a friend, "As we grow closer, I feel uncomfortable keeping a secret. I want you to know what happened. I'll feel better about myself and our relationship by sharing this." Or, you might say, "I don't want to burden you, and I don't want you to feel like you need to take care of me. I have an excellent therapist who helps me cope. But I do want to feel accepted for who I am."

You might share with your confidant about how your past experience explains certain aspects of yourself today. For instance, you might say, "You've noticed that I have a strong startle reaction. That's the result of PTSD from the accident."

You can invite your confidant to ask questions, either at the time of your discussion or at a later time.

You can also put some boundaries around the conversation. The transition to another topic might feel awkward, but you can say, "I'm willing to talk more about this, but for now let's enjoy our meal."

Despite our very best efforts, sometimes these conversations are disappointing. We don't feel the relief we hoped for, or the relationship might feel more strained. This is a time to support yourself. It does not mean that you should never tell anyone ever again. It might be useful to review the conversation with a counselor.

We want to be very clear that we are not advising you to share your story indiscriminately, go public, or confide in even one single person if you don't want to or don't feel ready. We are recommending that you consider if or how secrecy is affecting your well-being and your relationships. If keeping a secret is taking a toll on you, we recommend careful thinking and consultation with a pastor or therapist. And, if you do decide to open up to family or friends, be clear about what you want to share and why.

Contacting the Victim's Family

Has anyone ever contacted the family of the victim many years after the accident? Every day, I wake up thinking about the man I accidentally killed (thirty years ago) and his widow. I would like to apologize to her again and let her know that I have not forgotten. —Dorothy

About seventeen years after my accident, I reached out to one of the children of the father I accidentally killed in a car/motorcycle accident. The daughter I sent a letter to (typed and signed snail mail) didn't respond. But her younger sister, now a grown woman, responded to me via email in a very positive and forgiving manner. I almost instantly felt a lot of the weight lift off of my chest. I still feel guilt/shame and deal with the repercussions of living so many years with it, but it is much more bearable... I wrote her back, but she didn't respond. My feeling is that the victims will never be your friends and you won't be close, but you are still intertwined with them for life. It's a difficult cross to bear, but at least I don't feel the level of guilt, shame, and self-hatred I once did. I would suggest reaching out. The victim's family might not respond in the same way, but I think the act of reaching out in and of itself would be good for you. I'd say be prepared for anything. Stay strong! —Dennis

I saw my therapist a couple of hours ago and talked to him about how I planned on returning to the cemetery today and finally leaving an apology letter in a bottle and a flower on the stone. But then I got afraid. What if a loved one thinks I have no right going there and gets very offended and I cause them more pain? —Les

I feel absolutely responsible for the accident and want to talk to the injured victim to express my sorrow and apologize, and yet I also dread the possibility of this conversation. Would she yell at me and tell me how hard her suffering has been? Does she know how horrible I felt then and how horrible I still feel? Does she care? Does it matter? Maybe I would only be apologizing to make myself feel better. —Martin

A couple of months ago, I decided to reach out to the victim's brother and sister. His parents had passed away. I was nervous. I told them that the last thing I wanted to do was cause them any more pain. The sister and I have begun a little bit of a friendship. She has told me repeatedly that she has forgiven me. I cannot describe what those words mean to me. The brother was polite but a little more distant. I have not had much communication with him. Maybe if he's ever interested, someday, we'll talk. —Teresa

Soon after the sister and I began communicating a little bit, the victim's aunt reached out to me. As it turns out, she lives in the same county as I. We met for coffee. She was very gracious and forgiving. She encouraged me to get on with my life and to take care of my family. All this happened shortly before the holidays. I celebrated differently this year. —Kathy

Four—The Emotional Toll

Many Fellowship members long to express their feelings of sympathy, sorrow, and regret to those most deeply affected: the victim's family (or the surviving victim). They feel a strong desire to express remorse and sorrow and to let the family know that they care deeply. This longing can go on for years.

Despite how the surviving victim and/or victim's family responded initially, be aware that their response may change over time. Early expressions of understanding and forgiveness can harden to anger—or vice versa. The family is grieving and trying to address a variety of emotional and practical issues. Their preferences and feelings will evolve.

Many, perhaps most, lawyers will urge you not to contact the family. Their concern is that you might inadvertently say or do something that can be used against you criminally or civilly. Sadly, this silence can be painful for all involved, but it is important to listen to your lawyer.

Once the legal issues are resolved, there is no easy answer as to whether you should contact the victim's family. At best, there is forgiveness and healing. At worst, old wounds are opened or even deepened.

If you want to contact the family, it's essential to ask yourself why. Are you hoping the family will forgive you or at least assure you they understand you did not intend harm? Are you hoping they will recognize that you, too, have grieved and suffered? Are you hoping they will let you comfort them?

If so, be prepared for the possibility you won't get what you want. The victim's family has been on their own journey. Anger, vulnerability, and self-protection may be part of that journey. They might not want to meet with you, or they might choose to express anger and blame. That is their right. They are under no obligation to offer forgiveness or understanding, now or ever. The burden is on us, as those who have unintentionally harmed, to respect their feelings and preferences. Before making contact with the family, make sure you feel strong enough to accept a different outcome than what you want. Disappointment is to be expected under such circumstances, but if rejection would be devastating, we suggest waiting.

If you choose to proceed with contacting the family, we offer a few suggestions. First, consider writing a letter or an email rather than calling or stopping by. This allows the family time to absorb your message and consider how they want to respond rather than putting them on the spot to react.

Second, consider asking a pastor or someone else to act as an intermediary to approach the family and ask if they want contact with you, without pushing them one way or the other.

Third, keep the focus of your message on them and their grief. Avoid asking for forgiveness (or anything else). For instance, here's the letter that Maryann wrote to her victim's mother:

Dear Mrs. __:

I have thought about writing to you for many years but did not want to cause you distress. Thirty-one years ago, this past June, I was driving the car that hit and killed Brian. The way tragedy can strike in an instant is something we both learned that day.

To say I am sorry seems inadequate. I want you to know that not a day in my life has gone by when I have not thought of Brian. He lives on in my heart, as I know he does in yours. In tribute to him, I try to be a kind and good person.

I returned from a trip to Jerusalem last week. While there, I followed a Jewish tradition and selected a Hebrew name.

In Brian's memory, I chose the name "Bracha," which means "blessing."

I hope the years have brought you some measure of peace and joy. You are always in my thoughts.

Sincerely,

Maryann

Ask a friend to review the letter and offer some feedback to make sure the tone and message are consistent with your intentions.

Different considerations apply when you know the victim's family. If they are or were friends, relatives, neighbors, or co-workers, the choices you face are different and, in some ways, more difficult. In addition to guidance from your lawyer, we highly recommend asking mutual friends or a neutral party (e.g., a pastor) to serve as an intermediary.

You cannot control how your words of caring and kindness will be received. We hope you will find reconciliation, acceptance, and understanding. But no matter what happens—if you speak from the heart, with integrity and compassion, you will have done the best you can, and you can take comfort in that.

Key Takeaways

● Many of us feel guilt, shame, or embarrassment because of the incident, and these feelings may last for years. The challenge is not to rid ourselves of our emotional reactions but to manage them so we are not controlled by them. We need to acknowledge these feelings as a sign of our humanity and caring—and then channel that energy in constructive directions.

Discussion Questions

1. What kind of feelings do you have when you think of the incident? List them all without judging yourself or whether you have the "right" to feel that way.

2. Do you believe everything happens for a reason? Has the incident changed that belief?

3. Have you thought about the concept of "non-moral guilt?" What do you think about the idea that our guilt can be a sign of caring and connection to others? How can you transform the feelings of guilt into signs of emotional health and wellness?

4. Is your secret getting in the way of intimacy, community, or happiness? What is the difference between secrecy and discretion? What does that mean in concrete terms for you?

5. Have you considered drafting a letter to the family of the person you injured or killed? Whether or not you send the letter, writing a draft might help in your own healing process.

CHAPTER FIVE

Trauma and Spirituality

Looking back, I should have been killed in the accident too, which made me feel shockingly guilty...that I survived and the other man died. However, I have since realized that God preserved me to fulfill his plan for me, to help as many souls as possible. —Tyrone

If you've tried to make sense of your unintentional harm through theological lenses, like Tyrone, then you've done what the vast majority of us do: turn to something greater, both outside and inside ourselves, for guidance and meaning.

Why? We are what scholars refer to as *homo religiosus*: we are by nature inclined to look to a force outside of ourselves, beyond time and space that, by our very inclination, also suggests that a part of us is spiritual. Previous eras would have used the term "powers" to define one that creates, guides, gives purpose, and judges. "All men," said Homer, "have need of gods."

When we refer to spirituality, we are referring to a component of the human experience. Our spirituality is a part of who we are, a connection to that which transcends the self. This connection might be to God, a higher power, a universal energy, the sacred, or to nature.

As the saying goes, no one is an island. While the temptation to isolate and hide our pain and experiences from others is strong, tapping into that which is beyond as well as deeply within—our higher power—can make all the difference. We believe that recovery from unintentional harm is found not in ignoring spirituality but in embracing and leaning into it.

A Little Background

Scientists tell us that sometime over the past 200,000 years, humans, as we have come to know them, started evolving quite differently from their ancestors. Gradually, we became quite unique.

Today, we are the only animals who behave like we do. One of the biggest differentiators is that we wonder. We wonder about our relationships, about nature, and about our interior lives. We are the animals who make complex plans. We are the only ones who worry about the future. We are unmatched in our gifts as meaning-makers, looking for reasons and causes.

Over the last 10,000 years, this sense of wonder has become the basis for what we now know as philosophy and religion, as humans uniquely ask: Who are we? Why are we here? What are we supposed to be doing?

Soon, the idea of gods or God came to be, upon whom we could praise or blame for things that happened beyond our understanding. Some see the idea of God birthed from within, where God has placed a benevolent spirit that has fueled humanity's altruistic streak of caring, sharing, and loving. Others believe our ideas about God serve more as a vehicle of our own projection than as proof of the existence of a deity. As the French philosopher Volatire famously said, "In the beginning, God created man, and ever since, man has not ceased in returning the favor."

Nonetheless, we have been thoroughly unable to dismiss this natural tendency to wonder, make meaning, and sense a divine "Being," and thus, we turn to religion.

The world is awash in religion. By some estimates, there are 10,000 varieties of religions, and the vast majority of the 108 billion or so people who have ever lived have been religious, with some type of connection to the idea of God as creator, sustainer and hope for the future.

Surveys consistently find that most people endorse a belief in God or higher power. A 2022 Gallup Poll revealed 81% of respondents indicated a belief in God. Many of these individuals describe religion or spirituality as the most important source of strength and direction for their lives. Given that spirituality plays such a significant and central role for so many people, it is not surprising then that an individual's spirituality is often affected by trauma—and impacts the survivor's reaction to trauma.

We Are Communal

Our health is nearly always dependent on others. Very often, that "other" is our higher power.

When people experience trauma, especially the trauma of unintentional harm, some return to their spiritual or religious roots. Some flee from them. But eventually, nearly all of us seek sources outside of ourselves to give us the strength, guidance, and encouragement we need to keep going. Many of us, sooner or later, find that we cannot deal with the pain of our suffering by ourselves. We hit rock bottom. We need help.

Unintentional harm is a lonely affair. The shame, guilt, and unsavory nature of causing an unintentional death motivates us to bury, avoid, and even deny our pain. Deep down, we realize our lives might be happier and more fulfilling if we tried different strategies, but we are leery to reach out to those who might help us, even though asking for help is always the first step in getting better. That help often begins by calling on our higher power.

Our Higher Power

Some people use the name God, as we have previously indicated, to identify the higher power in their lives. Others use Buddha or Vishnu or even a group of people, like other members of the Hyacinth Fellowship. A friend of ours in Alcoholics Anonymous looks to that group as his higher power and says his G.O.D. stands for "group of drunks." Maybe you are not religious and have no notion of what a "higher power" is for you. That's okay, but we firmly believe that spirituality can be an important element in recovery and healing.

When we name our higher power, we admit that we cannot transform alone. We need assistance. Calling upon a higher power requires humility, which is essential to our healing. We must be humble enough to admit our mistakes. We must be humble enough to seek a therapist or at least talk to someone about our unintentional harm. We must be humble enough to speak candidly about our experiences, to be a light and hope to those who have unintentionally harmed. And we must be humble enough to seek forgiveness—from other people, from our God, and from ourselves.

Unsurprisingly, we often find that self-forgiveness is the biggest hurdle facing those who commit unintentional harm. In taking a human life, we have committed a major sin and coping with the repercussions is no easy task. Our transgression becomes the backbone of painful, sticky thoughts, haunting memories, even recurring nightmares.

Our difficulty in forgiving ourselves is not all bad. As we have noted in previous chapters, our guilt is also a sign of our goodness, our empathy, and our true intentions to seek no harm. We hold ourselves to standards of civility and kindness that are to be acknowledged and appreciated. To forgive ourselves too easily makes us question the depth of our self-awareness and our loyalty to these altruistic ideals.

In coping with these core feelings and beliefs, Maryann and I have discovered that our unintentional harm offers seeds for transformation. What we do with those seeds directly impacts our ongoing recovery.

Unintentional Killing and Transformation

Within 24 hours of the accident, I knew I had a simple choice: to either let this ruin my life or to somehow find a way to become a much better person than I ever thought I could be while finding a way to pay the universe back for what I took: the life of a wonderful, joyous, beautiful, talented, intelligent, and creative girl. I like to think I chose the latter. Almost every day, I think about my responsibility, and I try to make a positive difference in the world. —William

Unintentional killing can trigger a descent into darkness, often the deepest darkness we have ever known. We can no longer pretend we are in control of our lives. And we often find that the usual ways we cope with such pain simply do not work. So, we turn, or turn again, to something outside of us. This turn may not have come easily. We may have seen it as a sign of weakness or a character flaw. But when we finally reach out for help, to another person or to God as as understood by us, we can find that, in this surrender, comes the help we were waiting for.

It is not surprising that a large number of people who unintentionally harm go through a transformation of sorts. We often hear reports of people who have spiritual experiences, draw closer to God, are more aware of a divinity around them, or become more compassionate people. By nature, we change, and many people use their trauma to change, as much as it is possible, for the good.

We may also discover two transformations at play: the first at the moment of our unintentional killing and the second as we are re-made by our trauma. This second transformation may come all at once or gradually. Very often it involves something outside of us—our higher power.

This second transformation often takes us down the road of "Why?"

Trauma and Meaning-Making

At some point after your accident, you will engage in the natural process of meaning-making. You will ask: Why was I in that place at that time? Why did circumstances come together in such a way to produce this outcome? Why am I the one shouldering this burden?

We ask these questions, and we search for answers. But we live in mystery, a place where suffering never makes perfect sense. Nonetheless, we ask, and we search as we seek to make sense of our trauma.

The theological parlance for this concept is theodicy, a term coined by an eighteenth-century German theologian. Theodicy explores the age-old question, "Why do bad things happen to good people?" We'll look at seven paths that most of us travel as we seek to make sense of our traumas.

Everything happens for a reason

Those who experience the trauma of unintentional killing often identify with the explanation that God is in control of everything and that what happened did so for a reason. This theory is founded upon the assumption that God is all-seeing, all-knowing, in absolute control, and has reasons for bringing things about that humans cannot grasp. People who adhere to this belief will point out the positive things that happened as a result of their tragedy, (i.e., a greater awareness of life's fragility or an increased understanding of the love of our supporters). This, of course, makes God to blame for our tragedy—but a God whose mind is far higher than ours.

Free will

Many people who are uncomfortable with a God who causes harm often claim that since a God of love cannot harm, it is people and uncontrollable forces that cause/d the harm. They cite free will, the idea that a loving God gives people the freedom to make their own decisions regardless of the consequences. Adherents to this idea say that God is not responsible for the mistakes humans make. This, of course, does not totally absolve God from evil because the source for all that is still rests upon God. So, while God is not responsible for evil, God is still responsible for the possibility of evil.

Trauma as training

Approaching our tragedies with our eyes on our own well-being is at the heart of the idea that sees trauma as training. This theory says that evil is like a grain of sand in an oyster and will ultimately make us pearls through painful agitation. It's a "no pain, no gain" philosophy that sees human life as a training ground to better ourselves and the world. As we know, great works of art are often founded in suffering—from music to sculpture, poetry to film—so it follows, in this thinking, that tragedies can enliven our creative energies. Many people who espouse the trauma as tragedy approach believe God is closer to those who suffer. This theory begins to waver, though, when you look at incidents like the Holocaust or the Inquisition, times of such enormous tragedy that it can be heard to imagine any "training" as good.

We live in a war zone

Some people make sense of their tragedies by citing the existence of the devil, demons, and a life-and-death war between good and evil that's invisibly taking place in our midst. The idea that humans are involved in conflict between superhuman forces is not uncommon. Those who hold to this theory believe that our tragedies do not come from God but from nefarious forces seeking to drag God and all good things down in defeat. From this perspective, we do not suffer because God wants us to but because we live in a war zone. A significant question behind this theory, however, is: Why would God create such a universe, especially if God, inevitably, will be the victor?

We are partners

This theory posits that God has made humans as partners to enjoy and repair the world. Out of immense love, God has elevated humanity to partnership status. Humans can make crucial, life-altering decisions that God will honor. This means that God does not know the future, only the breadth of possibilities that can arise as free humans make their various choices. This frees God from the responsibility of evil and points to God's desire to suffer with and for people in order to equip the world to heal and reconcile. Those who criticize this theory believe it limits God and elevates humans to places that are too lofty.

Atheism

A number of people gaze upon the randomness of the world, the violence, suffering, and the absence of adequate answers and conclude that there is no God. The severity and comprehensive nature of suffering make this theory very attractive. How can any sort of loving God be at the helm of such a violent universe, where species come and go and humans inflict incomprehensible pain and oppression on one another? Those who adopt this position are understandably irate about injustice and suffering. A counterargument from religious believers is that this rage is only possible because of an objective moral standard. What makes us angry at the injustice and randomness? A divine source of ethical order. Thus, a central argument against God actually points toward God.

Our ways of coming to terms with our incidents within the framework of our spiritual beliefs will be as varied as the individual. In addition, as we have already noted, some people find a spirituality that does not require faith in the existence of God. Indeed there are forms of Buddhism and Judaism that are consistent with atheism in this sense. We invite you to pause and reflect on the ways you are making meaning of your incident. How are you addressing the "why?" questions? Which answers make the most sense to you?

Cities of Refuge

As we've seen, it is not uncommon for those who have unintentionally killed to fear they may be punished for inadvertently taking a life. You might find some direction from an inspiring story of care and compassion found in the way the ancient Hebrews dealt with unintentional harm. They did so by establishing something called Cities of Refuge.

Since the beginning, humans have unintentionally harmed one another. The Bible details a whole system set up to deal with these tragedies.

According to the Hebrew scriptures, particularly Numbers 35:6-34, Deuteronomy 4:41-43, 19:1-13, and Joshua 20:2-9, immediately following an unintentional killing, the "manslayer" fled to the closest of six Cities of Refuge, where he was safe from attack by the relatives of the victim, called the "blood avengers." In one of these cities, the perpetrator stood trial before an assembly. If the assembly agreed the killing was unintentional, the perpetrator returned to the City of Refuge, where he was required to live until the death of the high priest in Jerusalem. At that point, whether it was ten days or twenty years later, he was allowed to return to his home and live in peace.

Biblical commentary provides even more detail. For instance, to make sure the unintentional killer could safely reach the City of Refuge, the roads leading to the cities had to be twice as wide as a regular road and free of obstacles. The cities themselves were medium-sized—not so big that blood avengers could sneak in unnoticed but large enough for a perpetrator to find work. Rather than being relegated to a ghetto and shunned, the unintentional killers took part in all aspects of community life. In fact, they could even receive honors and high office in the city as long as they disclosed their status as unintentional killers.

But why was someone who killed unintentionally required to live in a city of refuge even though he did nothing wrong?

There's the obvious need for asylum, since the victim's relatives may be angry and vengeful for quite some time. Some scholars have also noted that the safety of the city allowed an unintentional killer to move beyond fear of the blood avengers to a deeper consideration of life, death, and personal responsibility.

Another puzzle is why the unintentional killers were allowed to leave the City of Refuge when the high priest died. One rabbi writes that the death of the high priest reminded everyone that no one lives forever, so the victim's family would realize they were not alone in their grief. This rule also takes the uncertainty out of the question of when to "move on" with one's life. It wasn't a moral or psychological issue but rather a legal and societal issue.

While Cities of Refuge don't physically exist in our modern world, that doesn't mean we cannot create them for ourselves. Ask yourself:

- Where is your safe place?

- Where do you feel distant from bullying or revenge?

- Where can you think deeply about what your incident means and how you want to respond?

The answer may be in a church, mosque, or temple. Perhaps in a therapist's office, at a beautiful mountain lake, or maybe at home with friends and family who love you.

Living with our tragedies is transformative whether we like it or not, and, for many of us, it's an invitation to positive spiritual change and practice. Has your incident prodded you to take spiritual belief and practice more seriously?

Engaging with Your Spiritual Side

Engaging our spiritual side is often a foundational component of working toward wholeness. You may be inclined to use your trauma to develop or redevelop your spiritual life. We have found the following framework helpful. It's based on four pillars: meditation/prayer, affirmations, positive influences, and altruism.

For many people, our spiritual lives are the foundation of who we are. So, finding a practical and fulfilling way to develop or improve this central part of us in light of our incidents can be critical to our ongoing recovery.

Meditation/Prayer

What we mean by meditation and prayer is a way to center. It is a time to both talk and listen to our own heart and to the voice of Another. Prayer can include confession, praise, thanksgiving, petition, intercession, and centering. Many people draw up a list of people or situations to pray for. Some people pray while walking or driving; some set aside quiet time in the morning or at night. Some people pray silently; others use words out loud rather than spontaneous or written prayers. The point is to take some time to commune or communicate with our higher power as a way to center ourselves.

Affirmation

Affirmation is about immersing ourselves in nurturing words. This could take the shape of repeating a list of positive statements or regularly reading sacred texts like the Bible. Our brains sometimes lie to us and tell us we are less; we are not enough, and we are inferior. We are our worst mistake. We look to important words and statements of truth to remind us of who we really are, what our purpose might be, what's being asked of us, what we are capable of, and what our best selves can look like.

Positive Influences

Developing a healthy spirituality also means monitoring the influences around us. While researchers say we are the sum total of the seven people closest to us, we also need to look at all the influences in our lives, including the books we read, the websites we peruse, and the podcasts we listen to. Our incidents may tempt us to look to unhelpful ways of coping, like drugs and alcohol. These and other negative influences offer a way to cope that is ultimately harmful. Maybe your parents once told you that bad company corrupts good morals. In this case, good company produces good people.

Altruism

Developing a positive spirituality always includes altruism, which means doing good for others. When we wake up in the morning and think less of what we need and more of what others need, our problems become minimized, and the world is helped by our charity. While our altruism can take many forms, we have found it helpful to include assisting others who have unintentionally harmed. We believe that helping those who have done as we have can be restorative and healthy in many ways. Centering on others before ourselves is a time-honored way of healing.

Key Takeaways

* Successfully coping with unintentional harm is a spiritual endeavor involving humility, surrender, and transformation. We highly recommend that those who have unintentionally harmed others seek out ways to use their spirituality to help them feel and do better.

* As we turn to a higher power in this journey, we have the opportunity for transformation as we make our way to healing and wholeness.

Discussion Questions

1. What role did a higher power play in your life before the incident? What role does a higher power play now? If there's been a change, reflect on the reasons behind that change.

2. In the trauma and meaning-making section, we discuss seven different paths or approaches. Which one resonates most with you? Why?

3. In light of the Cities of Refuge story, name your safe place (and/or person). Where do you feel distant from bullying or revenge? Where can you think deeply about what your incident means and how you want to respond?

4. Which of the four spiritual pillars do you already practice? How might you engage in one of the others?

CHAPTER SIX

Taking Care of Yourself

I am from Northern Ireland. I am 42 years old with three great kids and a husband I have adored for the last twenty years. I buried my dad two weeks ago, and yesterday, I hit an elderly woman with my car. I was pulling out of a parking lot onto a main road, and one minute, there was no one there, and the next minute, there she was. She was injured, and I still don't know how badly, and I have never felt anything like the shame and guilt I feel.

I feel like I'm dying inside. I pray to God she will live and that I will not have taken this mother away from her family. But I feel like no matter what happens, my life is over...done and dusted, and I'll just be an empty shell. The thought of my children, my husband, and my poor mum having to deal with me is just too much to bear. My head is full of images of the woman hitting my car on repeat and my dead dad lying in a hospital bed...the two images alongside each other go round and round like a washing machine. Will this ever stop?
—Carey

The pain of unintentional harm can be absolutely devastating.

Our incidents tend to leave us defenseless against our own recriminations. We harbor intrusive thoughts and say terrible things about ourselves, things we would not even reserve for our worst enemies, let alone those we love.

Many of us believe that those who have died or been injured because of our actions want us to live our lives as consciously and compassionately and as best we can. In order to do that, we must learn to forgive—both others and ourselves—and do so with deep gratitude.

Moral injury, post-traumatic stress, and the other maladies we've explored so far in this book are painful. We can't just shrug off the bad feelings and the dark thoughts. But we do need to find a way to care for ourselves.

Permission

Our first challenge is giving ourselves permission to care for ourselves. So many who have unintentionally harmed tell themselves they do not deserve to feel better, ask for support, or expect anything other than just getting by. One member wrote, "I'm not the victim, so I don't deserve help." We disagree.

Guilt and distress are normal and appropriate after causing harm. But even though you feel guilty and ashamed, even though you may have made a terrible mistake, you can still treat yourself with compassion. You can feel badly without condemning your entire being. All the energy that now goes into disparaging and punishing yourself can be channeled in another direction: honoring the victim(s) of the accident, appreciating the precious beauty of life, and living a life of purpose and meaning.

Our feelings of grief, fear, anger, remorse, and whatever else are just feelings. There's nothing wrong with having them. But it's what we do with those feelings that matter.

We can never make up for taking a life. No matter how many good deeds we do, we can't wipe the slate clean. We can, however, do our best to make restitution or reparations—if not directly to the victim's family, then to others. We can resolve to honor the memory of our victim in the way we choose to live from here on out.

The four steps from offense to reconciliation are acknowledgment, apology, reparation, and reconciliation.

■ Acknowledgment is truth-telling. What really happened? Can we arrive at the facts of the incident?

■ Apology is the admission of the facts and the expression of sorrow and regret.

■ Reparation is the tangible expression of our apology and can include actions, possessions, words, and deeds. While never an adequate substitute for a life taken, reparation can express the depth of our desire to fix what we've broken.

■ Reconciliation is always out of our control because it requires the consent of both parties. We must understand that those we've harmed have no obligation to forgive or seek peace with us. While the odds of reconciliation can improve over time, finding ways to cope with current reality remains important.

Moving through these steps becomes much harder, if not impossible, when we're in the grip of PTSD, moral injury, or other mental health problems like depression or substance abuse. These ailments leave us living smaller, more constrained lives. Fear keeps us from taking risks or reaching out. Shame keeps us isolated. Intrusive memories and grief sap our energy. We turn inward, and we turn on ourselves, and that can block our healing.

You may have made a terrible mistake, but that does not make you a terrible person. We are all more than our accidents; in fact, our distress is evidence of our caring. We are hurting. Let's acknowledge our whole self, not just our mistakes, and allow ourselves solace and permission to take care of ourselves.

How would you treat a friend who unintentionally killed someone? Would you tell them they're a horrible person who deserves to suffer forever? Or would you remind them that they are a loving, caring person who did not intend harm? Would you show them that you love them by sticking by them and offering a hug, a listening ear, and a kind response? Treat yourself the same way you would treat this friend.

We recommend that you receive professional psychotherapy or counseling. Therapy does not mean you're weak, crazy, self-indulgent, turning yourself into a victim, or whatever other reason you might be giving yourself for avoiding it. It means you are taking care of yourself.

Here's what a good therapist will offer: First, relief from PTSD symptoms such as intrusive images, difficulty concentrating, feeling numb, or negative emotions. Second, they will help you find ways to cope with your symptoms and feelings so that you can work, parent, and, in general, function more effectively. Third, they will offer support so that you can feel less alone and get some relief from distress and misery. Fourth, a therapist can help you manage anxiety, guilt, and shame so that you can think more clearly and make better decisions about how to respond to the accident. Fifth, a therapist can help in dealing with relationship issues that the accident either caused or worsened, including relations with your spouse or partner, parenting, and other friends and relatives. Sixth, the therapist can work with you to clarify values, goals, priorities, and plans.

Therapy can relieve pressure on your family, who may be struggling with their own worries, fears, and grief (what psychologists call secondary trauma.) You may be withholding some of your thoughts and feelings from your relatives or close friends because you don't want to burden them, don't think they'll understand, or don't give yourself permission to share them. And they might be withholding thoughts and feelings from you, not wanting to add to your distress. The result is a lonely gap. Therapy can help you close this gap and regain emotional intimacy.

A licensed therapist (or someone working under the supervision of a licensed therapist) offers strong confidentiality and privacy protections for you, but they are not unbreakable. They are mandated to report to authorities if you disclose that you have abused a child or an elder; they are also mandated to report if you express an intention (as opposed to a fantasy or wish) to harm or kill someone. Many will also intervene if you are at immediate risk of suicide. This is also true for ordained clergy in many states.

In the U.S., the courts generally respect the confidentiality of a licensed therapist. While it is very, very unusual for courts to mandate licensed therapists testify about their clients, it can happen. For example, if you are charged with a criminal offense and part of your defense involves your psychological condition or mental well-being, your therapist may be compelled to testify. If you are or might be involved in litigation, we recommend that you talk with both your therapist and your attorney.

Keep in mind that an unlicensed therapist does not have the same protections. For that reason, be careful if you choose to consult a psychic, an unlicensed therapist, or a peer counselor. The courts may not consider your conversations with them to be confidential.

As we have mentioned in earlier chapters, talking with a pastor or spiritual advisor can also be helpful. Clergy are generally well-versed in discussing faith components but may not be well-trained in dealing with some of the other psychological issues common among those who have accidentally killed or seriously injured. Ideally, you would be in conversation with both a clergy person and a licensed therapist.

If you're opposed to seeking therapy, we urge you to reconsider. But if it's not for you, there are peer support and self-help resources, many of which we review later in this chapter.

Types of Therapy

As you may have discovered, "therapy" covers a wide range of methods and experiences. Some have been studied; many have not, so their effectiveness is unknown. Here, we review some of the approaches to treating trauma and/or moral injury that research has found to be effective.

Cognitive Processing Therapy (CPT)

The American Psychological Association strongly recommends Cognitive Processing Therapy (CPT) for treating PTSD. CPT is most often applied in twelve sessions of individual therapy (private sessions between you and the therapist). It can be used in group therapy as well, which generally is less expensive and allows you to learn from and with others. CPT focuses on our beliefs, because these beliefs are at the center of our trauma reactions. The American Psychological Association explains on their website that "changing the content of cognitions about a trauma can impact emotional and behavioral responses to the trauma."

A therapist using CPT will first make sure you understand the causes and symptoms of PTSD. They will ask you to talk and write about what happened, in part because we so often try to avoid aspects of our traumas, which can end up prolonging PTSD.

Then, the therapist will invite you to clarify and express your thoughts and feelings as well as how they are affecting your relationships and behavior. Sometimes, we just feel numb and have difficulty identifying our thoughts or emotions; other times, it seems like we are all over the emotional map and need help understanding how our thoughts are contributing to our PTSD and negative emotions.

The next step will be to explore and gently challenge problematic beliefs such as, "Only a bad person would do what I did," or "I can never be happy again." As you recognize and accept alternative beliefs, you will learn skills for applying this form of reasoning to other aspects of your life.

Through CPT, you will confront painful experiences in a safe and supportive setting, you will learn to combat unhelpful and inaccurate beliefs and thoughts, and you will develop stronger coping skills. Feelings of depression, anxiety, shame, and guilt should decrease so that you feel better and function better in daily life.

CPT requires homework. You will be asked to write the story of your accident and its impact on your beliefs about yourself and others. You will likely receive worksheets or other assignments each week so that you can continue to work on applying what you've learned in each session to your life. During the sessions, you will discuss the homework as well as other issues relevant to trauma.

Prolonged Exposure Therapy

This is another form of cognitive therapy that focuses on your thoughts in order to treat PTSD. It is especially helpful if fear and avoidance are strong elements of your PTSD. Exposure therapy involves facing the traumatic memories and the emotions the memories evoke rather than avoiding them. Generally, this is accomplished in a series of individual sessions.

After discussing what PTSD is and how it has been affecting you, the therapist will ask you to close your eyes and tell the story of the accident (or other trauma) in as much detail as possible. This often includes a detailed sequence of events as well as what you were thinking and feeling and sensory memories such as what you heard, saw, felt, or smelled. As you do this, the therapist will ask you to subjectively rate your distress at various points in time. Even when your distress is high, they may encourage you to keep going. Often, the therapist will record you and ask you to listen to the recording in between sessions. This is called "imaginal exposure" because it relies on imagination to face the trauma.

This task is repeated over and over: you keep telling your story as the therapist listens and asks questions to elicit more memories. And you continue reviewing the story in between sessions.

Although sharing all this detail about the trauma is scary and upsetting, it cuts through our tendency to avoid painful memories so that we can face and master our anxiety and related feelings. Our subjective ratings of distress decline as we tell the story over and over. We learn that we are strong enough to face the memories, that nothing terrible happens when we remember, and that we can manage our emotional responses.

In addition to imaginal exposure, your therapist might assign you "in vivo exposure" as homework. In vivo exposure means facing what we fear or want to avoid in real life, not just in our imagination. However, this is done in a gradual way to ensure that you do not become overwhelmed or flooded with negative feelings and memories. Instead of returning immediately to the accident scene, for example, you and your therapist might come up with a list of related settings for you to visit, so that you can manage your anxiety and work up to whatever is most frightening and distressing.

Although Prolonged Exposure Therapy can be scary, a strong body of research supports its effectiveness, and the methods have been refined over years. The American Psychological Association also supports this approach to treating PTSD.

Other Cognitive Behavioral Therapies

We have focused on CPT and prolonged exposure therapy because of their particularly strong evidence base for trauma. But other forms of cognitive therapy and cognitive behavioral therapy can also be effective and are strongly recommended by the APA, especially when delivered by a therapist who has experience treating trauma and PTSD.

Eye Movement Desensitization & Reprocessing (EMDR)

This has become a popular and increasingly well-regarded method for treating trauma. The American Psychological Association offers conditional approval of EMDR, but most of the other major mental health organizations, including the American Psychiatric Association, fully support it. The Department of Veterans Affairs also endorses EMDR. Psychologists disagree about how or why it works, but a growing body of evidence indicates that it does work, and that's what matters to us.

According to the International Association for EMDR website, "EMDR therapy, rather than focusing on changing the emotions, thoughts, or behaviors resulting from the distressing issue, allows the brain to resume its natural healing process. EMDR therapy is designed to resolve unprocessed traumatic memories in the brain."

During an EMDR session, you may be asked to describe aspects of the trauma as well as your thoughts related to the trauma. As you do so, the therapist will lead you through eye movements, which help to reduce distress while you remember the trauma and stimulate the brain's healing capacities. Through this process, you will also come to replace negative beliefs with more positive beliefs. Unlike CPT and Exposure therapy, EMDR does not generally include homework assignments.

EMDR practitioners are specially trained and certified—not every licensed therapist knows the techniques and methods. If you are working productively with a therapist who does not do EMDR, you can talk with them about EMDR as an addition to your ongoing therapy. The combination can be very effective. Most practitioners consider EMDR to be short-term, requiring a limited number of sessions (about a dozen, although it can vary).

Phases of EMDR

Phase 1: History & Treatment Planning (1-2 sessions). The therapist learns about the client and establishes a treatment plan based on specific "targets" such as past events or present stressors.

Phase 2: Preparation (1-4 sessions). The therapist builds a relationship of trust with the client, explains the EMDR theory and process, and teaches relaxation methods that the client can use at any time to deal with emotional upset.

Phase 3: Assessment. The therapist and client focus on a particular target. The client identifies a thought that accompanies the target (e.g., I am helpless or I am bad), considers a positive thought that they would like to replace it with (e.g., I am capable or I am a good person), and rates the subjective feelings and reactions that arise in relation to both the negative and the positive thoughts.

Phase 4: Desensitization. The therapist leads the client through eye movements, taps, or sounds while the client talks about a particular target and related thoughts or associations. This is intended to stimulate the brain in specific ways to help the client more fully process the memory so that the brain can heal from trauma.

Phase 5: Installation. This therapist continues to help the client strengthen positive beliefs and release negative beliefs. Skills training or other interventions may be needed to help the client believe that the positive beliefs are true.

Phase 6: Body scan. The client explores with the therapist if any residual tension remains in the body when remembering the target event. If so, further work may be indicated.

Phase 7: Closure. Ending the session with a sense of progress and equilibrium with teaching the client and self-calming tools for use as needed in between sessions.

Phase 8: Reevaluation. Opens each new session, allowing the therapist and client to revisit the treatment plan and refine it as needed.

Source: Experiencing EMDR Therapy | EMDR International Association (emdria.org)

Somatic Experiencing (SE)

Somatic Experiencing is another method for treating PTSD that is not based on talking about your trauma. Instead, SE strives to activate and strengthen our natural healing capacity. Although research supports the effectiveness of SE, most of the major associations have not yet endorsed or recommended it. In part, this is because it is not necessary to be a licensed psychotherapist to be certified as an SE practitioner, so make sure you understand the background and credentials of the practitioner you select. (And, if you are involved in litigation, keep in mind that an unlicensed practitioner does not have the same strong protections for confidentiality that a licensed therapist has.)

SE is based on the work of best-selling author and psychotherapist Peter Levine, who wrote about how we get stuck in a "fight, flight, or freeze" response as a result of trauma. In short, our bodies continue to act as if we are still facing threats to survival long after the incident is over. SE helps us release this stored energy in order to resolve the traumatic reaction and enable us to become more resilient and less rigid in our responses to stress.

SE helps us release this energy slowly, in little bits over time, not in one giant explosion (or implosion) that can be overwhelming. It is a gentle process. The idea is to stay in the "here and now." The SE therapist will help you become more aware of your bodily sensations, your breath, and where or how you are holding tension in your body. As you focus on the body, you may find yourself releasing energy through trembling, other "micro" bodily movements, or emotional release. Over time, as this stored energy dissipates and the body is no longer locked into a "flight, fight or freeze '' posture, you will feel more vital and less controlled by trauma. Your abilities to regulate your emotions improve, and you will be better able to manage life's inevitable stressors.

Some SE practitioners may ask you to describe your trauma so that you both can explore your body's reaction to these memories and release the stored energy. Unlike exposure therapy or CPT, however, SE approaches this slowly. You might begin by describing the day before the accident, or you might share bits and pieces of the story. Over time, you will be less anxious and distressed when you talk about the accident.

You should feel safe and comfortable with your SE practitioner before the work of energy release begins. This work takes place in a regular therapy office. You remain fully clothed. You can sit in a chair, although your therapist might invite you to lie down if you want. The therapist might offer light touch only (and only with your permission). Their touch should not be intrusive in any way.

Other Choices

There are other options for treating PTSD including Acceptance and Commitment Therapy; Narrative Exposure Therapy, Brief Eclectic Psychotherapy, Stress Inoculation Therapy, and Psychodynamic Therapy. You can explore these online. Many therapists use a combination of methods, and you can also choose multiple methods, such as adding EMDR or SE to talk therapy. Regardless of the therapeutic approach you prefer, your therapist should be licensed (or an associate working under the supervision of a licensed therapist), and you should feel safe and comfortable with them.

A note about medication: When anxiety, depression, insomnia, or other negative emotions are getting in the way of your functioning, medication may be helpful. Today, there are many options, and new drugs are introduced every year.

However, the first line pharmacological treatments for PTSD remain serotonin reuptake inhibitors which include selective serotonin reuptake inhibitors (SSRIs), such as fluoxetine (brand name Prozac) or sertraline (brand name Zoloft), and serotonin and norepinephrine reuptake inhibitors (SNRIs), such as venlafaxine (brand name Effexor) or duloxetine (brand name Cymbalta). Perhaps conveniently, these medications are also the first line of pharmacological treatment for anxiety and depressive disorders. Be prepared for some trial-and-error before finding the right medication(s) and dosage(s) for you.

In most cases, it is best to see a psychiatrist who is up to date on the science and can monitor your reactions to the prescribed drugs and refine the prescription as necessary. However, a primary care provider can also prescribe psychiatric medication, and this is a good option for many people if a psychiatrist is not available.

Medication is most effective when combined with therapy. It is not a substitute for therapy, but it can help you make better progress in therapy. Provided you give permission, your psychiatrist and therapist might want to talk with one another so they can work together for your well-being.

If you are reluctant to take medication, talk with your therapist or primary care doctor. The idea is to make sure that you have accurate and complete information before closing this door.

If you have a history of drug or alcohol abuse, or a history of other medical or mental health conditions, it is essential that you share this with the doctor.

Finding a Therapist

To find a therapist, we suggest asking trusted friends and family members for referrals. If a therapist you contact is unable to see you, they should be able to offer a referral. Other people to ask include your pastor or your doctor. If your employer has a confidential employee assistance program, you can obtain some short-term counseling from them, and most will help you find a referral to a qualified therapist.

Therapists work in a variety of settings. In the U.S., Health Maintenance Organizations (HMOs) typically offer counseling as part of their available services. Other health insurance providers will offer a list of therapists that are in their network. Many therapists, however, prefer to work independently, outside of these networks. If they are not included in your insurance plan, you may get only partial or even no reimbursement from your health insurance plan for the costs of therapy.

Almost all therapists in private practice have some kind of web presence. You can find those near you by reviewing therapist finder sites listed online. We recommend you do some research to make sure the therapist is licensed and in good standing.

Most communities in the United States offer mental health services on a sliding scale based on income (including free). Some services are offered by city, county, or state departments of mental health; some are offered by private non-profit clinics. You can find these on the web. Schools and graduate programs that train therapists also offer low-cost services.

Finally, there has been a rapid increase in online therapy providers in recent years. This service tends to be less expensive than traditional private practice and is convenient, provided you have a private time and place to hold a session. It is great for people who live in rural areas, are homebound, or lack easy access to a therapist. You can find dozens of online providers on the web.

Finding a *Good* Therapist

A considerable body of research indicates that the key to successful therapy is not the technique or the method but the relationship. You should trust, respect, and feel safe with your therapist. You should feel like they listen to you and respect you. You should feel like they are able to sit with you in your pain and anguish. And you should feel like they have expertise and knowledge that will be helpful to you.

We have already written that your therapist should be licensed. In the U.S., this means they have had sufficient training, supervision and experience to practice independently, and they have demonstrated their knowledge by passing a rigorous test. Continuing education is required as a condition of maintaining the license, so a licensed therapist is up-to-date on advances in psychotherapy. They are also required to adhere to a rigorous set of ethical standards. A less costly alternative is to meet with an intern or associate—a therapist in training who is not yet licensed but is working under the supervision of a licensed therapist. In the U.S., each state has its own requirements and standards for licensure. Someone licensed in Pennsylvania cannot treat people in Maryland or Virginia.

Licensed therapists generally have either a master's or a doctoral degree. Psychiatrists have medical degrees. In our experience, it doesn't matter all that much if the therapist is trained as a social worker, marriage and family therapist, clinical or counseling psychologist, or psychiatrist. The degree they hold tells you little about their skill as a therapist.

Psychiatrists are the only mental health professionals who can prescribe medication. However, they are not necessarily highly skilled in talk therapy, and they are usually more expensive than other therapists. Most therapists can refer you to a psychiatrist for a medication consultation if needed.

We suggest meeting or talking with two to four therapists before selecting one. They will ask you about your needs and goals, and they should be comfortable with you asking questions. Here are some questions you might ask as you choose the best therapist for you.

- What kinds of licenses or certifications do you hold? How long have you been practicing?

- Have you received any special training in treating psychological trauma or moral injury?

- What is your experience in treating people with PTSD or other trauma reactions?

- I recently had a serious accident, and someone was killed (or seriously injured). Is there anything in your background that might make it difficult for you to hear about this and support me?

- How would you describe your approach to therapy? What kind of theoretical orientation underlies your work?

- Are you available for telephone conversations, text messages, or emails in between sessions, if I feel the need?

- How often should we meet (once a week is usual, but some therapists will recommend that you meet more often in the beginning, especially if you are in crisis)?

- How much do you charge?

Some therapists will answer personal questions, such as whether they are married, what their sexual orientation is, or if they have kids; others will not, at least not until they explore with you why that's important to you.

A number of people have told us that they refused therapy because they could not find a therapist who had experience in treating people who have accidentally killed or seriously injured. We have found that relatively few therapists have this type of experience—but that does not mean they are unable to understand and help you. What matters most is their ability to listen with compassion, share their knowledge and understanding of psychological trauma, and work with you to reduce troubling symptoms, thoughts, emotions, and behaviors.

Very few therapists know about moral injury; most are not even familiar with the term. That says more about the state of research and clinical knowledge than it does about a particular therapist. You can tell them that there is a moral dimension to your pain that you would like to talk about with them. Their response may give you a good sense of their openness to discussing these issues.

Here are some things a therapist should not do: take a phone call in the middle of your session (unless there's an emergency); touch you in a way that feels uncomfortable or sexual or make comments that are inappropriately sexual or seductive; push you to do something you are not ready to do (with the possible exception of Prolonged Exposure Therapy); violate confidentiality (except for conditions discussed earlier in the chapter); ask you for a personal favor; or treat you more like a friend than a client. If this happens, talk with the therapist about your reaction and consider making a change. Sometimes, a therapist will say something that feels "off" or insensitive. It's best if you can share your reaction with them. Repair is possible and can strengthen the relationship, but if this happens regularly, you may need to look for another therapist.

A good therapist will be by your side as you journey from trauma to peace and growth. They will be there to witness your struggle, offer compassion and understanding, and help you accumulate the insights and skills that will hasten the journey. You deserve this support.

Self-help

We can supplement the support we receive from others with self-help. These days, you can find hundreds of self-help books, articles, and websites on trauma, anxiety, depression, personal growth, and virtually any other topic you can think of. It can be overwhelming. How should you proceed?

First, the warnings: be careful of self-help resources that promise or "guarantee" quick fixes, especially if they are trying to sell you something. If it sounds too good to be true, it probably is. Be careful of resources that advise you to turn away from traditional methods, such as therapy, counseling, or psychiatry. Be careful of self-help websites that want you to pay upfront and/or collect all kinds of personal information. Be careful of resources that present a particular person as the be-all and end-all, one who is so gifted or talented that they are sure to heal you.

On our website, www.hyacinthfellowship.org, we offer a few suggestions, but there are many, many more. Here we describe a few of the options.

Self-help for PTSD: We suggest browsing online or in a bookstore to select a book that appeals to you. Many offer useful exercises and describe techniques for calming yourself in response to triggers, examining your beliefs, and regulating your mood. All of this can be helpful, and we encourage you to pursue this path but keep in mind that if self-help worked reliably, a lot of therapists would be out of business.

Self-Compassion: Because so many of us are very hard on ourselves, information about self-compassion and self-forgiveness is important. There are a number of excellent websites, books, and articles. Kristin Neff, co-author of *The Mindful Self-Compassion Workbook*, says, "Self-compassion is a practice in which we learn to be a good friend to ourselves when we need it most—to become an inner ally rather than an inner enemy."

Neff and several other experts in this field describe exercises that we can do on our own in order to increase our awareness of the ways we undermine ourselves and build new skills for supporting ourselves. We recommend that you look into these.

Expressive writing and other forms of artistic expression: Expressive writing helps us heal from trauma and moral injury. Hundreds of research studies have shown it to be effective in improving mental and physical health. John Evans, a psychologist who focuses on expressive writing, described it this way: "Expressive writing comes from our core. It is personal and emotional writing without regard to form or other writing conventions, like spelling, punctuation, and verb agreement... it simply expresses what is on your mind and in your heart."

Expressive writing lets us gain some distance from our thoughts and feelings. We can see ourselves more clearly, and that helps us be less reactive and to ruminate less. We can see what obstacles are getting in the way of our healing.

If writing is not your thing, you might want to express yourself in other ways, such as through art, music, or crafts. Such forms of creative expression can also provide perspective and relief. Allow yourself to experiment with different forms, creating a collage, for instance, taking a pottery course, or pulling out that guitar that's been neglected in your closet for the past few years.

Grounding: Among the more troubling aspects of PTSD are dissociation and depersonalization—the sense that we are removed from ourselves or looking at ourselves or others from afar. Some people say they feel "spaced out" while others describe feeling numb. We may find that our mind is blank, or we are besieged with images and memories of our trauma. Those experiencing dissociation find it impossible to stay in the "here and now" for periods of time This can be upsetting and can interfere with work and relationships. By searching the web or a local bookstore, you can find dozens of exercises for grounding ourselves and "coming back to earth" when this occurs.

Many grounding exercises are quick and simple. One member told us that she used to wear a rubber band around her wrist. When she felt herself dissociating, she learned to snap the rubber band against the back of her hand, literally "snapping back to reality."

Physical activity: Movement and exercise can be calming, regulating the arousal that is often part of PTSD, and helping us regain a sense of control. There is ample evidence that exercise is associated with a better mood and less depression. If you are not used to exercising, start with gentle movement such as a beginning yoga class, a stretch class, and/or going for a daily walk. Some forms of exercise, like swimming or jogging, are repetitive and meditative; others, like dance or boxing, require you to place your attention in the "here and now." Choose whatever activity calls out to you, because you are most likely to persist if you enjoy it. It is not necessary to join a gym or hire a trainer; the web and YouTube are loaded with options.

Mindfulness: The UCLA Mindful Awareness Research Center defines mindfulness as "the moment-by-moment process of actively and openly observing one's physical, mental and emotional experiences." According to Tara Brach, an expert in mindfulness, "The capacity to witness what is happening inside us with a non-judging attention allows us to respond to life from our full intelligence and heart"

The UCLA Mindfulness Research Center reports that mindfulness has numerous benefits, including:

- Less tendency to ruminate

- Fewer negative emotions like depression, anxiety, or fear

- More positive emotions

- Better concentration

- Better sleep

- Improved physical health

Mindful awareness is generally associated with meditation, but meditative practices such as yoga can also promote this state. The web and your local bookstore are full of resources to learn different mindfulness methods.

Roughly 10% of people with PTSD find that meditation has negative effects. For these people, it leads to intrusive images and bad memories and can actually increase stress. Almost all beginners feel some anxiety when they first try to meditate, such as an increased heart rate or difficulty settling down. If this feeling does not go away after several sessions or if you feel a high level of distress, try signing up for a meditation class but keep in mind that meditation might not be a good strategy for you.

Peer Support

People who have experienced severe trauma often benefit from talking with others who have had similar experiences. Such conversations offer a level of understanding and empathy that few others can offer, and they can have practical benefits as well such as sharing information and suggestions for coping. One commenter explained it well:

> *Ever since my accident, more than 10 years ago, I never talked with another person in a similar situation until I came here. It's amazing to talk with someone who truly understands what it's like to go through this. I don't feel so alone anymore.* —John

Adding to the difficulties that we face is that opportunities for peer support are limited. Most of us have never talked with another person in the same situation because we tend not to mention our accidents in casual conversations at work, church, social events, etc. There are few support groups, chat rooms, or other settings for us to gather.

We are working to change this. We offer three opportunities for peer support.

Fellowship meetings: Each month, up to 40 people gather online for 90 minutes in order to listen, learn, and, if they wish, share in a safe and compassionate setting. Most fellowship meetings are organized around a theme, such as post-traumatic growth, self-compassion, or moral injury. The opportunity to interact in this way is powerful and healing.

Expressive writing meetings: You can do expressive writing on your own, as we described in the self-help section above, but writing in a group has special benefits. When we are writing about painful and traumatic events, it can be comforting to look up and see others engaged in the same activity, rather than to write alone and then, once finished, still be alone with the experience. In addition, when we debrief with others about the writing experience, we gain support and extend our learning.

One-to-one peer support & mentoring: Many of us have initiated informal contact with others in between fellowship and expressive writing meetings. To make this option available on a broader basis, we are making it easier to seek support from peers on an individual, one-to-one basis. Peer supporters have learned valuable lessons about trauma, coping, and growth through their own experiences, which they are willing to share. The relationship between peers gives both parties opportunities to learn and grow.

Note that none of these peer support opportunities can substitute for professional counseling or therapy. They are, however, great additions.

Something like this is extremely difficult to deal with, and, for me, it was one of the hardest things I've ever had to deal with in my entire life... What I did was I immediately sought counseling, which was very scary but helpful in the end. There were also a lot of helpful books and, of course, God. It was also very helpful to speak with other people who have gone through the same thing, which is why this website has brought a lot of comfort to me. There's not a day that goes by where I don't think of the accident or the man that I killed, but I have learned to move on and to be happy again.
—Michelle

Key Takeaways

* The pain of unintentional harm can be absolutely devastating, but we are not defined by the worst moment of our lives. Just as we would treat others who have accidentally killed with compassion and understanding, so too should we offer that love to ourselves. Taking care of ourselves can mean a number of things, from talking with a therapist to work through our feelings of shame and guilt, to adopting practices like meditation or developing peer supports.

* We can never make up for taking a life. No matter how many good deeds we do, we can't wipe the slate clean. We can, however, do our best to make restitution or reparations—if not directly to the victim's family, then to others. We can resolve to honor the memory of our victim in the way we choose to live from here on out. Taking care of ourselves is an important step in that journey.

Discussion Questions

1. Are you reluctant to focus on self-care? Why? What are some of the key messages in this chapter about the importance of taking care of yourself?

2. The four steps from offense to reconciliation are acknowledgment, apology, reparation, and reconciliation. Where are you in this process? Which step is the most difficult? Do you experience this process as linear or an ongoing cycle of healing and recovery?

3. If you are reluctant to seek a therapist, spend some time thinking about what is holding you back. Write down some of those obstacles, and then look for some solutions.

4. What kind of self-help practice appeals the most to you? What is beneficial in that practice? What other types of self-help practices might you try?

CHAPTER SEVEN

Caring for Someone Who Has Unintentionally Harmed

At age 17, my son accidentally shot and killed his very good friend. It was ten days before his eighteenth birthday, which he spent in jail. We are still trying to figure out how to live with all this. It has been two months since the accident. He has lost some of his friends who think he was irresponsible and guilty and still has some who give him strong support and know his heart. He has changed completely from who he was before. He used to be loud and liked to joke around, make people laugh, go out, and have friends over. Today, my son doesn't leave his room, doesn't sleep at night, doesn't sit with us for dinner, and sometimes, he doesn't even shower. He's waiting for his court date, and he keeps saying he deserves whatever it comes. I not only worry about him going to jail but also about his mental health. It's like he's broken, and I can't fix him. —Helen, mother

My husband accidentally hit a pedestrian, and she died four days later. I am having a hard time finding any information online to help my husband through this. He is constantly filled with guilt and blame and many other things, I'm sure. He doesn't talk very much and just zones out, so I usually just give him space. I am hoping I can get advice from others on how to help him through this. —Trina, wife

My dad overcorrected and rolled his car, killing my uncle in the passenger seat. I don't know how to help him emotionally. I was wondering if any of you guys had any suggestions on how I can help him. He blames himself and I don't know how to ease the guilt. —Andrew, son

---

Our children, spouses, and loved ones...we would gladly trade places when suffering and pain come along. So, when someone we love has unintentionally killed or injured someone, we want to help them through the pain. But often, we don't know what to do or how to help.

Perhaps your situation is similar to this scenario.

You are happily going about your day when you receive a call or heard a scream. Your spouse, child, parent, friend, or neighbor has been involved in a fatal event.

The next few hours are a blur of activity. You have to call for an ambulance or administer aid on the scene, or you're trying to figure out what happened and why. Your friend or relative may be emotional and need calming; they might seem out of it or unresponsive. They might also have physical injuries that need attention. And then there are the practical issues: getting the kids home from school, telling your boss about a family emergency, and getting whatever information you can from police or others on the scene.

Someone you love has done the unthinkable. They are in devastating pain, maybe the worst of their lives. And because we love them, we are too.

Now what?

Supporting someone who has committed unintentional harm is challenging. There are so few resources to guide you. Your compassion and concern for them compete with anxiety and fear about what the future holds. Will there be an arrest? A civil suit? Will there be media coverage? How should you handle this with the kids? Will your friends and neighbors be understanding or blaming? You might also feel angry with your loved one. How could they make such a terrible mistake? They may have jeopardized your family's well-being.

In the short term, you have two main responsibilities. The first is helping your loved one. The second, and equally important, is supporting yourself. Let's look at each of these.

Helping Your Loved One

(Advice from someone who has committed unintentional harm): My husband was my rock. He didn't do anything. Seriously. He was his normal self. He helped me to see that life would go on, and it would continue to go on. My best friend came and watched movies with me. She cooked dinner and made coffee. She held me as I cried and said it didn't make me a bad person, just an unlucky one. I still struggle at times. It never goes away, but talking has helped a LOT! —Artemis

(Advice from the wife of someone who committed unintentional harm): Just be there and don't change. Your husband needs normal and ordinary as he comes to terms with extraordinary things that have happened to him. Your love, your faith, your shoulders and arms, he needs you. These things seem like they only happen to other people,

to everybody else, but I am the other person and so is your husband. Encourage him to talk but don't give platitudes. You will cope, and so will he. —Edna

(Advice from someone who has committed unintentional harm): My advice to you as a parent is to make sure your son is seeing a professional therapist who deals with this all the time—even when he says he's fine and doesn't need it. Trust me, in 15 or 20 years, you don't want to be sorry you didn't. —Kyrika

---

As the loved one of a person who has unintentionally harmed, you are in a unique and important position.

Personal support is one of the most powerful tools for coping and healing after trauma. Many of those who commit unintentional harm fear they will be shamed, rejected, and cast out of their families, communities, and friendship circles as a result of unintentionally harming someone. Simply reassuring them that you love and accept them and that you are not going to abandon them is vital. Research shows that early encounters with respected people (you!) often play an outsized role in how the event is perceived and processed. Know that your positive presence, in word and deed, is very important and may play a pivotal role in your loved one's recovery.

As we know, even when your beloved is overwhelmed by trauma, life goes on. The children need help with homework, the bills need to be paid, and everyone has to eat. Your help with these mundane tasks will make more of a difference than you know. Your loved one is having to cope with these everyday tasks as well as the new responsibilities and obligations that come with their event of unintentional harm. This is not to mention the emotional challenges they are facing. Your assistance in helping carry an incredibly burdensome load can make a big difference and is a great way to show that you care.

Let's flesh out what this might look like.

Providing Emotional Support

I remember things got pretty intense with my husband. He didn't really want me to talk about what happened. One day, I burst into tears. He asked what was wrong, and I told him I didn't understand why I couldn't talk to him about it. He said it's just that I'm afraid you're going to cry, then it'll make me cry, and I don't want to cry. We hugged it out, but I told him he was the only one I wanted to talk to about it. —Hazel

Just two days ago, on New Year's Eve, my boyfriend was driving home from the coast when a driver unexpectedly crossed all three lanes on a highway and directly into my boyfriend's vehicle. They were coming from his left, and the wife in the passenger seat was instantly killed. Two little boys also passed away later. He is struggling with the guilt, and I don't know how to help him. He also struggles with all of the "what if's." Telling him he's wrong to feel guilty is the first mistake I've made. I didn't say it in those words of course, but the message was the same. He is becoming frustrated with others telling him that it's not his fault. He knows it's not, but he still can't stop feeling guilty anyway; his words: "My car hit their car, and people died. Two little boys died." While I don't know the feeling, I can understand it. What do I say? —Lynn

---

In the shadow of a serious event of unintentional harm, the first and perhaps most important thing your loved one is looking for is emotional support. This means listening with love and acceptance while withholding judgment. It means offering a hug, a shoulder to cry on, or simply the comfort of your presence. If your loved one does not want to talk about what happened, don't push them. Just being with them may be enough. If they want to be alone, try to balance respecting their wishes with letting them know you are available.

As a clergy member, Chris is often asked how emotional care is best rendered in situations like this. People who have caused unintentional harm need to hear three things from us:

First, they need validation that what they're going through is bad, that this is a tough time, and that their feelings of emotional pain, responsibility, guilt, and shame are not abnormal. One of Chris's friends received a bunch of cards in the mail when word got out about her unintentional killing, and the only one she saved was from a 10-year-old girl that simply read, "Oh no!" Grieving people need to know that their pain and hurt is okay.

Second, your beloved needs to know that you care. You can tell them that you love them or that you care for them, but they also need to know that you are concerned and bearing the load with them. Not visiting, calling, or texting is a cop-out. Find a way, in word, deed, or both, to express the fact that you care about them. As the saying goes, grief shared is grief lessened.

And third, your loved one needs to know that you are there for them, that you're present. You can choose to be in a lot of different places, but you have chosen to be with your loved one in their time of sadness. This may entail watching a silly movie with them or taking a walk together. If your loved one is reluctant to leave the house or be seen in public, don't push them but offer to accompany them to the supermarket or gym. If they are afraid to drive after a car crash, offer to go with them when they first get back behind the wheel; if they are afraid to go back to work after an occupational accident, see if you can help arrange for a sympathetic co-worker to greet and be with them when they first go back. Being there for them is one of the most important ways you can offer emotional support.

Those are the three important things. That's it.

Avoid the temptation to try to fix things. Don't say: "It could have been worse," "God needed this to happen," "God's teaching you something," or "This happened for a reason." The subtext of these comments is "Stop feeling bad!" These are common responses because no one likes to be around hurting people. Consciously or unconsciously, we don't say these things for their comfort but for ours. Put your loved one first. Don't try to fix it. First of all, you can't fix it, and secondly, no hurting person wants to hear these things.

You may be tempted to join a chorus of people who are saying, "It wasn't your fault!" This may be true. It may be corroborated by verifiable evidence. But more than likely, your loved one is not ready to hear or accept this. In fact, for many of us, it can take a long time to look at what happened as the accident it was. Your attempt to convince them of this ahead of its time may be perceived as uncaring and another "fix it" gesture that is unhelpful at best.

Sometimes, family members don't want to hear their loved one talk about their feelings or fears. This can be upsetting to hear, or they may believe that the person needs to "buck up" and not "give in" to grief, guilt, or trauma. They may also be angry with them for disrupting the family so profoundly. These reactions are entirely understandable, and there is nothing wrong with them, but they are not helpful to either your loved one or the family. If your loved one wants to talk about their worries, try not to cut them off or argue, which will leave them feeling more alone. Your willingness to listen and offer sympathy and affection are important. This approach will help your beloved become better able to manage their feelings, think clearly, and resume their day-to-day responsibilities.

Providing Practical Support

My brother is going through this. Just a few weeks ago, while he was putting a gun away, it went off, hitting and killing his girlfriend, the woman he planned on marrying... a lot of people blame him. He has serious PTSD now, continually reliving the moment. He can't sleep, he hardly eats, and loud noises make him cry. People are saying he needs to rot in jail instead of comforting him over this misfortunate accident. I'm constantly fighting them on Facebook when they call him a scumbag... I don't like it, but when I tell them they're wrong, they come after the rest of my family, telling us we are mentally unstable and that he deserves to rot for his entire life. I see my brother daily... he's a broken version, someone who's hurting, and I can't do anything about it. He will never be the same. —Diane

---

The brokenness many of us feel when we unintentionally harm cannot be overstated. Supporting your beloved, then, may also include practical, tangible support. What errands need to be run? What household tasks can you take care of for them? Would they like you to call their employer, talk to the insurance company, or inform the in-laws? Does your loved one need help in finding a therapist or a lawyer? Can you screen social media for them? Your help can allow your beloved to focus on getting stabilized.

A note of caution: be careful to get the okay from your loved one before jumping in with these or other tasks. Traumatic experiences put us in touch with our helplessness and the limits of our ability to control ourselves and the world, so your beloved might be especially sensitive if they feel you are taking over.

Your loved one may also need informational support. You may be called upon to be a trusted pipeline for important information about the event and subsequent support.

What does your beloved need or want to know? They are likely to have questions about the victim and the victim's family, about any legal or insurance issues, and about their post-traumatic experience, feelings, and thoughts. Many people who commit unintentional harm worry about the reaction from friends, family, and community, including social media and media coverage. Use your judgment in responding to these requests for information. If social media is harsh, for instance, perhaps you can offer to screen the posts or suspend the accounts. If your loved one is struggling with symptoms such as intrusive images or flashbacks, difficulty concentrating, or emotional swings, you can remind them that these are common responses to trauma and not a sign that they are crazy or breaking down.

Although you and your loved one may be very anxious to hear about the condition of the victim in the days following an accident, be aware that the victim and their family have a right to privacy. Hospitals do not disclose information about their patients, and law enforcement may or may not know or choose not to share such information. As much as you and your beloved care about the victim, recognize that neither of you has "rights" to this information.

Providing practical support may also include basic coordination and organization. If friends and family are asking, "What can I do?", perhaps you and your loved one can come up with a list of assignments that would be helpful, such as babysitting or helping with transportation (see the worksheet in Chapter 2). In addition, some accidents generate considerable paperwork and require burdensome tasks, such as keeping track of medical expenses, dealing with a damaged car or equipment, working with an insurance company, pulling together information for an attorney, and so forth. This can be overwhelming, especially when each task carries an emotional component. If you're a good organizer, you may offer to help set up files or make sense of the paperwork. This can save time and stress.

To the greatest extent possible, allow your beloved to be in charge of their own healing and to make their own decisions. This does not mean you shouldn't offer your input. It means recognizing that your loved one is capable. One of the most painful elements of a trauma is the sense of helplessness it engenders because we are confronted with the fact that we are not fully in control of ourselves or our lives. Restoring a sense of efficacy and agency is important.

A Few Exceptions

There are some exceptions to these general guidelines. First, if you believe your loved one is suicidal or at risk of hurting themselves, it is time to intervene. You can call the suicide prevention lifeline and ask for help (or encourage your loved one to do so), you can bring your beloved to a local emergency room, or you can contact their therapist or doctor (or encourage your loved one to do so) for crisis intervention. If possible, stay with your beloved and offer your love and compassion.

If your loved one is abusing alcohol or drugs to escape their pain, intervention is also warranted, up to and including making arrangements for them to enter an addiction treatment program. The trauma of unintentional harm can push people over the edge and those with a predilection toward substance abuse can be at particular risk. Keep a close, loving eye on them!

Taking care of your beloved is particularly fraught for parents who are trying to help their teenage or young adult child after an accident. The normal tensions between adolescents and parents can be ramped up, sometimes causing the child to turn away or reject parental support. At the same time, parents typically ache for their child and want so badly to relieve them of their despair.

Professional counseling for your loved one is appropriate, but if they refuses, then the parent(s) should consider counseling for themselves to discuss how best to address the child's needs.

You are not responsible for making your loved one feel better or relieving them of their guilt. It is so hard to see those we love suffer, but suffering is inevitable. What you can do is validate their pain, be with them in their suffering, and show them they are loved.

Your compassion is an awesome gift. However, it can take a toll on you, which brings us to your second responsibility as you support your loved one.

Taking Care of Yourself

Family members and close friends of those who commit unintentional harm experience their own stress and trauma. You grieve for the victim and their family. You also grieve for the toll this takes on your beloved and others (e.g., the children, parents, or other loved ones on the periphery). If you were at or near the scene of the fatality, you may have some of the post-traumatic symptoms we've described, or you might feel traumatized by the way in which you found out about the accident. As one of our Fellowship members has said, "This doesn't just happen to you. It happens to the whole family."

Yes, there are all kinds of worries. Will your beloved ever recover from this, or will they be forever scarred? Will they be arrested? Will they go to prison? Will you lose the family savings in a lawsuit? Will the media coverage or social media chatter affect the kids or provoke retaliation against the family? It is not unusual to feel angry as well. You know your loved one did not intend harm, but their actions caused tragedy, and the results are life-changing. And as you hold your anger in, others rush to cruel judgment, even if they don't have all the facts.

On top of that, supporting your beloved requires energy to take on extra tasks, help coordinate or plan, and find the strength to sit with them and listen.

The case is still outstanding. We are continuously reminded to lay low by our lawyer. My son has not been charged... but where we are today is in holding, waiting... The waiting is tearing me apart. I keep trying to plan for the worst, and my heart is ready to fall out of my chest with the weight of anxiety....He's in therapy, as am I. He has to take sleeping pills to keep the nightmares at bay. He goes to school and does his best to forget about it each day. But it's there. It's everywhere, as we wait. "This too shall pass." The waiting will end. But until then, it's killing me. It's tearing me down with worry. My anxiety is at an all-time high. It was an accident. I know this. In my heart, I know it. But will the prosecutor see what is clearly in front of him? Only time will tell. —Lashanna (mother)

Things were building up, and my husband seemed upset all the time. I talked to my therapist about it, and she said, "Maybe you could try to talk to him. Tell him you're sorry for all the stress and extra expenses, and you'll make it up soon as you can get back to work." So I did and he said, "It's not the money. I don't care about that. It's that I drive my truck for two weeks in a row. The last thing I want to do is drive all over when I get home." I had lost my license because my friend and I had been drinking the evening of the accident. We lived out in the country, and I had friends who helped me out with a lot of rides for drug and alcohol groups and AA meetings... But when he was home for a week between each trip, he'd take me. I didn't know it was stressing him out like that. Once we talked about that, things seemed better. —Lucy Clare

---

Secondary traumatic stress is the desolation and anxiety that comes from hearing about the fatal accident and doing your best to support your loved one (or others involved). Another term for secondary trauma is "compassion fatigue," which implies how much energy it takes to support someone in crisis. Secondary trauma can mimic certain symptoms of post-traumatic stress: emotional upset or feeling numb, difficulty concentrating, ruminating and worrying, or feeling overwhelmed and hopeless. Your sleeping or eating may be disordered, or you might have physical symptoms like an upset stomach or back and neck pain.

These are all signs that you need to take care of yourself. Seek social support from friends or relatives and take some time away from your suffering loved one to be by yourself or do an activity you enjoy. Exercise, time in nature, creative expression, meditation, and self-compassion exercises may also be helpful.

It is okay to have boundaries, even if your beloved is a close family member. Few people have the fortitude to be available around the clock, every day. Some tasks might need to be handed off to someone else so that you can find some breathing space and attend to yourself.

If your loved one wants to be left alone, you might end up feeling rejected. You reached out with love and compassion, and your gifts were refused. Remember that withdrawal is a symptom of moral injury, guilt, and shame. The urge to hide from others, especially those who we dread disappointing, can be powerful. In addition, pre-existing relationship tensions do not go away when a trauma occurs. However, this is not the time for big "relationship talks" or major decisions about a relationship. You can give yourself compassion and respect because you've done your best. Your hurting loved one may reach out to you in the weeks or months to come. Healing is a long-term process.

If compassion fatigue is interfering with your life, you might want to talk with a therapist, pastor, or counselor about your feelings and fears. Also keep in mind that, just as your loved one's anguish affects you, your feelings and worries affect theirs. By dealing with your anxiety and grief with a therapist or counselor, you will help your beloved stay calm.

Those who care for people who've unintentionally harmed are offering vitally important support. Even small gestures of acceptance, support, and caring can make a big difference. Thank you for reaching out.

DO

- Listen with compassion, if your friend or relative wants to talk.

- Offer to keep your friend or relative company if they do not want to be alone. Sometimes a quiet presence is very helpful.

- Offer to help with everyday tasks and errands including transportation, childcare, meal preparation, etc.

- Offer to help undertake tasks related to the accident, such as contacting the insurance company or finding referrals to psychotherapists, doctors, or attorneys.

- With permission from your friend or relative, contact his or her employer.

- With permission from your friend or relative, inform other friends, relatives, and neighbors about what has occurred and, if necessary, coordinate support.

- Scan newspapers, television news, and social media so that your friend or relative is not blindsided by media coverage or posts on Facebook, Twitter, and so forth.

- Remind your friend or relative that flashbacks, intrusive memories, difficulty concentrating or remembering, emotional swings, insomnia, feeling dazed or "out of it," and other such symptoms are common responses to severe trauma.

- Be a proponent of psychotherapy, especially if their symptoms are severe or if they are still experiencing symptoms after 30 days. Similarly, psychotherapy or counseling may be helpful if your friend or relative is abusing alcohol or drugs to help them cope.

- Remind your loved one that you support them and believe in their ability to cope and recover. Remind them of their many strengths and capabilities.

- Ask your beloved what they need and seek their approval before making decisions or taking actions that affect them.

- Take care of yourself. You may also be feeling upset, frightened or even traumatized by this situation.

- As appropriate, support them spiritually with your prayers and presence. Share devotional books with them. Remind them that God has not abandoned them and is at work through the tragedy.

DON'T

- Do not push your loved one to talk about the event if they do not want to.

- Do not push your beloved to drive or take other steps that they do not feel ready for, even if you believe such steps would be helpful. Be a proponent of counseling or psychotherapy especially if your loved one is unable to resume most daily activities after three or four weeks.

- Do not offer drugs or alcohol to help your beloved feel better or relax.

- Do not tell others about the accident without permission.

- Do not discuss the accident with others over social media. Keep in mind that your posts could be used in unexpected ways, especially if there is criminal or civil legal action.

- Because people who have experienced traumatic events need to regain a sense of control and agency, be careful about offering too much advice or taking everything over. Encourage your loved one to make decisions and choices.

- Do not hold back from expressing your love and support.

Key Takeaways

* Personal support is one of the most powerful tools for coping and healing after trauma. But offering this support is not an easy task for the loved one. You, too, might be experiencing trauma, grief, or even anger. Find ways to take care of your yourself so you can offer the emotional and practical support your loved one needs.

Discussion Questions

1. What are some of the ways you can offer emotional support to your loved one who has accidentally killed or seriously injured someone?

2. What are some of the practical ways you can help?

3. How can you take care of yourself as you are trying to provide emotional and practical support?

CHAPTER EIGHT

Life After Unintentional Harm

I was diagnosed with PTSD a month after the accident due to the night terrors, lack of sleep, loss of memory, motivation, and emotions. My spouse and I did receive counseling from the college and the chaplain on campus. This experience, though incredibly tough and horrible to deal with, has made us into the strongest individuals and team. I just want to tell someone who has been in our shoes—or is going through it now—that things never are the same; however, they do get better! —Josie

---

Yes, this is the good news!

Coming to a place of sustained peace and solace is probably in your future. However, there is no timeline for recovery and healing after unintentional harm. We have found that the first year is the most difficult, but there is tremendous variation. Some people feel better within a few months; others struggle for years, especially if they are involved in long, drawn-out court cases or if the trauma of unintentional harm comes on top of other trauma.

After a while, your emotional injury will probably subside, even if it develops into PTSD or serious moral injury. You will feel more yourself again. You will be productive at work and engaged with family and friends, and you may go back to doing activities that you enjoy. Your friends and family will be relieved to see that you are doing well.

Getting to this place is both an achievement and a practice. Your hard work has led you to a space of peace and normalcy. Allow yourself to appreciate the strength and determination it takes to manage the trauma of unintentional harm. But realize this is likely a lifelong enterprise. Know that your continued health may depend upon doing healthy things. What habits and rhythms have you picked up along the way that have helped you get to where you are? What practices are in place that are serving as pillars? Take a careful look at how you got to where you are and make sure to leave the training wheels on long enough. It is not easy, but you have persisted and will continue to do so. This is cause for thanksgiving.

What might the more challenging days look like? You will probably still think about the victim, their family, the accident itself, and the aftermath. Sadness, guilt, or other emotions and memories linked to the accident may creep into your life, sometimes for just a minute or two and sometimes for a few days or weeks. You may still have an exaggerated startle reaction, and activities that used to come easily to you, like driving, childcare, or certain kinds of work, may now cause fear or anxiety.

On top of this, you might be reluctant to talk about the accident because you "should" be over it by now—or you're afraid that everyone is tired of hearing about it. So, when the dark days come, you resolve to simply endure them or manage on your own.

Even as you acknowledge the difficulties that still occur, make sure you recognize your own growth. None of us ever wanted to be tested in this way, but we have learned about our strength and resilience. We may have grown in compassion, commitment to our values, and our determination to live a virtuous life. We may be better able to accept support and to support others. We may be less quick to judge. We may be more engaged in community and doing our part to make this world a better, kinder, safer place.

In this chapter, we discuss the long-term consequences and challenges of causing unintentional harm. And these are not all negative! We will unpack something called post-traumatic growth, which is, in its complexities, as unexpected as it may be valuable. But first, let us consider two common and recurring hurdles you have already face: coping with triggers and marking the anniversary of your event.

Triggers

Tonight is the Fourth of July. I was driving home from watching the fireworks at the park, and I guess I was triggered by all the pedestrians as I was leaving the area. Once I got home, I just laid down and started crying. I haven't cried this hard since the night of the accident. I didn't know I was bottling up all this emotion, but I still feel so terrible. If anyone has some coping tips that they find work, please share them with me. I thought I was fine, but tonight made me very confused about where I'm at. —Mary

Nine years after my accident, I still have random thoughts of "You don't deserve to live" or "You deserve to die in a car accident." Sometimes I will just be walking or lying in bed and have a quick flashback. I have never told anyone of my struggles. Most of my friends don't know, and my family thinks I have "adjusted well" because I hide my emotions. —Ted

It's been almost a year since I ran over a lady who was laying in the road, most likely after being hit by another car... Everyone said it wasn't my fault and I just needed to get past it—and I kinda did for a while. I still thought about it most days though, and just last week, something happened to me. I was driving down that road like I had done many times. When I got to where it happened, I swear I saw her lying there again, and I felt like I couldn't stop. Since then, it has all come back to me. I can't sleep, and, when I do, it's nightmares and waking up randomly. Even now, I can just be sitting there, and it happens: I zone out, and I see it all over again... I can't talk to anyone, about it because no one gets it unless you've been there. —Lana

(From a Fellowship member who hit a pedestrian over 15 years ago) Two months later, my marriage fell apart, not from this circumstance but from other circumstances. So, I buried the accident down deep, never really knowing how to deal with it. But lately, it's been hitting me hard. I still remember all the smells of the evening. Looking at the sky and seeing the moon and wanting to drift away. —Tyreece

---

Wouldn't it be nice if the journey from accident to inner peace was a nice, straight line slanting upward? In fact, it's a jagged line with lots of ups and downs. Sometimes it circles back on itself. We may not see the upward slant until we gain the perspective of time.

A big reason why we have ups and downs is because certain experiences or events "trigger" us. A trigger is more than a simple reminder. It's an involuntary response that affects our emotions, thoughts, memories, and bodies. When we're triggered, our minds and bodies react as if we were back in the throes of the trauma.

For instance, imagine having unintentionally harmed someone in a car crash and having to regularly drive by the location, or seeing an accident vividly depicted in a movie, especially if you don't know it's coming. Certain sounds, odors, tastes, or emotional states might also trigger you. Sometimes we're not sure what the trigger is.

You might feel your back, shoulders, and neck tighten. Maybe your stomach starts to churn, or you feel yourself flushing. You're suddenly on high alert, feeling super anxious and jumpy, sad, afraid, angry, or sick with guilt. Your tendency to "fight, flee, or freeze" kicks in. A quick image of your accident flashes through your brain. Suddenly, you're no longer fully present. Your body is at work, home, or in the movie theater, but your mind is back with your accident. Your mood plummets. You are triggered.

The results of this trigger might last only a few minutes, or it might last for days. If it goes on beyond that, you are probably experiencing some delayed PTSD, which a therapist can help with.

Emotional States as Triggers

All kinds of emotional states can trigger your PTSD or moral injury. One that is especially common among Fellowship members is joy. Many of our members tell us that as soon as they start to feel really happy, something happens inside them to quash the feeling.

For instance, you might tell yourself that you do not deserve to feel happy or that feeling good insults the memory of your victim or their family. You might remind yourself that your victim will never laugh or smile again and that their loved ones suffered a terrible loss due to your actions. These and similar beliefs can spark negative feelings, difficult memories, and hopelessness about the future.

Even though these beliefs are irrational, they can carry tremendous power—especially if we don't talk about them. They can take root deep inside us, ultimately sapping our vitality and forcing us into smaller, more constrained lives.

It's important to recognize these triggers and to challenge them. Read about self-compassion. Talk about them with a therapist or someone who loves you. Refusing yourself happiness does not honor your victim. It only compounds the losses from the accident.

Dealing with Triggers

Yes, triggers will likely come, so what do we do? First, don't beat yourself up or tell yourself that you should be over this by now. Your body is doing what it was built to do as you continue to go through an unpredictable process. It's fine to confide in a family member or friend: remember, that little voice in your head telling you that everyone is tired of hearing about it or that this is your burden to bear alone is not your friend.

Second, try not to let the trigger send you spiraling down into hopelessness. Triggers happen; it does not mean you are crazy, forever scarred, or helpless. Again, these are natural processes many people experience and can remind us of the goodness of our humanity: we are kind, compassionate people at our core, and the lingering nature of our suffering points to our goodness. You can endure the anxiety, sadness, and guilt, and you can take steps to feel better. Understanding that triggers are "normal," even though they are upsetting, can help put things in perspective.

Here are a few strategies to consider:

Go to the body and the breath: When we start to feel spacey, removed from the "here and now," or in the grip of a trauma reaction, we can "get out of our head" and ground ourselves in the present reality with some simple exercises. You can find examples by asking your therapist or searching online.

Expressive writing: Use this method to put your thoughts and reactions on paper so you can put some distance between you and your trauma reaction. Expressive writing can help you identify triggers, recognize how trauma and moral injury drive reactions, and reconnect with yourself, especially your strength, character, and coping skills.

Social support: Talking to someone can defuse the triggering reaction. The conversation can give us perspective and enable us to see the trigger for what is: our brain playing tricks on us or an old set of thoughts and feelings that momentarily overwhelm us. A supportive friend, family member, or counselor can remind us that we are so much more than our trauma. They can also help us develop plans or strategies for coping with triggers.

Meditation and mindfulness: If meditation has been an effective strategy for you, use it when you are triggered to calm your overstimulated nervous system and return to or stay in the here and now.

Sometimes, we can anticipate triggers. For instance, we might be unable to avoid visiting certain places associated with our accidents. Making some plans can be helpful, and reminding yourself that you have coping skills and abilities can even lessen your reaction.

Fear of being triggered can affect your day-to-day life. Avoiding certain places or people because they are likely to trigger you is nothing to be ashamed of. But if avoidance, fear of being triggered, or frequently finding yourself triggered gets in the way of your full participation in life, we recommend talking with a therapist. A variety of techniques can mitigate these problems, sometimes in just a few sessions. Also, keep in mind that some people experience delayed-onset PTSD months or years after their accident. Again, that doesn't mean there's something wrong with you; it's how your body and brain deal with trauma.

Coping with Trauma Anniversaries

Anniversaries are among the most common and painful days of the year for those of us who have committed unintentional harm. There's something about these milestones that can bring back memories and re-stimulate our PTSD. While some Fellowship members are not distressed by the anniversaries, many members dread them.

Some will try to find a way to make the day meaningful and infused with hope. Many of us will attempt to deal with a traumatic anniversary by ignoring it or just "powering through," pretending that nothing is going on. Even when this looks like it's working, it probably doesn't feel very good. We know some people in our Fellowship use the anniversary as an occasion to remind themselves of how bad they are. Obviously, this is unlikely to serve any kind of positive purpose at all.

Another common strategy is to distract ourselves with work or other activities (i.e., binging on a TV show). It might seem like you're able to forget, but be alert to the subtle physical, mental, or emotional signs that your awareness of the date is lingering in the back of your consciousness and asking for attention.

Yet another way is to simply accept that the day is going to be sad and go about your regular routine, just plowing through and making the best of it. While this at least has the benefit of honesty, it is neither compassionate nor constructive.

We have a few suggestions on ways to make the anniversaries a little less awful—but it's important to know upfront that there is no right or wrong way to deal with trauma anniversaries, so long as you are not hurting yourself or others. You will have to find the coping mechanism that works best for you.

So here are a few other ideas to consider. Many of these come from a helpful website, Healing Well Counseling.

Mark the day: Instead of pretending to others (or yourself) that nothing special is going on, take the day off from work or other obligations. This is not the day to schedule an appointment with your tax accountant or hold a big meeting with your boss. It also might be a good day to avoid social media and/or news media. If you have unavoidable obligations, do as much advance work as possible to reduce your stress. Prepare a written agenda for the meeting with your boss, for instance, or make sure there are leftovers you can simply reheat for dinner.

Take care of yourself: Avoid drinking, non-prescription drug use, or other behaviors that do not contribute to your own well-being (like eating a quart of ice cream). Try to eat healthy meals, exercise if you can, and soothe yourself with soft music, gentle massage, a warm bath, or a walk in the woods or on the beach. Treat yourself gently and kindly.

Remind yourself how far you've come: Allow yourself to grieve for the victim and the victim's family and for all that you and your loved ones have suffered. Unintentional killing is, above all, sad. But also reflect on your own journey toward healing, from those first unimaginably horrible hours to wherever you are now. How have you grown and changed? What work remains to be done?

Honor your victim and yourself: Consider devoting the day to honoring the memory of the victim and everyone who has suffered. This might mean volunteering at a soup kitchen or clearing trash off the beach. You might plan to go to church or temple or write a letter to your congressional representative about accident prevention. You can also use creative expression to honor the victim: write a song or a poem, take photos of flowers in bloom, or create a collage.

Design a ritual: Some members of our Fellowship write a letter to their victim every year (some rip the letters up; some save them). We know some who say special prayers or go to places that deepen their spiritual connections (the beach, the woods, a museum, or a concert are all possibilities). Developing a ritual that acknowledges loss while reaffirming the beauty and preciousness of life can offer a powerful path to healing.

Allow yourself support: If you feel like spending the day alone, ask yourself if this is a form of punishment or a way to care for yourself. If it's driven by guilt, shame, or self-punishment, give yourself permission to find solace with others. Schedule an extra therapy session or a telephone check-in with your therapist; ask a clergy person to talk or pray with you, or share a pizza with a friend. This is not being weak; this is taking care of yourself.

As we take seriously our condition and recovery, putting into practice healthy habits and attitudes, many of us discover something surprising: growth.

Post-traumatic Growth

Within 24 hours of the accident, I knew I had a simple choice, to either let this ruin my life or to somehow find a way to become a much better person than I ever thought I could be while finding a way to pay the universe back for what I took: the life of a wonderful, joyous, beautiful, talented, intelligent, and creative girl. I like to think I chose the latter, and almost every day, I think about my responsibility, and I try to make a positive difference in the world. —Becky

In the fall of 1978, I was very, very fortunate in that I was entering a fine arts program in a distant city that trained professional actors. There, I was encouraged to get in touch with my emotions and express them honestly. Theater school saved my sanity. I have written and produced a play, songs, and a film about the accident, and, someday, I hope to make that film. I am now a published author and professional speaker, talking to whoever will listen about the need for respect, to respect others, and to be respected in turn. In fact, it seems that ever since the accident, my life has been a search for respect—respect for myself, which is the hardest thing to achieve after being accidentally responsible for the death of someone you loved. —Derek

I am, like so many of you, a survivor, burdened with guilt and shame and deeply cognizant of my own mortality. But I find the choices I have made and the work that I do to help others liberate me somewhat, freeing me up to be decent, kind, and caring. It's my victim's legacy, and I honor it completely. —Bruce

Even after I did everything I possibly could to turn my life around, there was still something missing, something I just couldn't get past so I could forgive myself. People would tell me, "I know you say you're okay now, but there is still something I can see in your eyes." Then, one day, I got a call from my old probation officer asking if I'd be willing to tell my story on the victim's impact panel for the county. I was scared to death, but I figured I'd give it a try. If it could help someone not to do what I did, that would be worth it. After I did my first presentation and heard all the good feedback, I felt a little better. Then the schools began to call. I've been doing my presentation for five years now, maybe two to four times a year and the results are very good every time. The students have helped me more than they'll ever know with their thank yous and hugs, and some tell me I just changed their life forever. A couple of years ago, I realized that I had finally moved forward. I'm not so afraid of what other people think because most are grateful that I'm telling my story. And now, I can finally forgive myself. The accident will always be there, and I'll always wish it hadn't happened, but I feel much better. —Luke

Although not charged with a crime, I lived with guilt and shame for decades, struggling to maintain normal relationships, employment, and sobriety. The turning point came when I became a registered nurse at the age of 40 and dedicated the next twenty years to helping others. With this work came a sense of purpose and self-regard that I hope will suffice for atonement and healing... I can't bring back the lives that were taken and forever changed, but I have helped others to achieve health and continue their lives. —Louise

---

The concept of post-traumatic growth is receiving a lot of attention from psychologists these days, but it's actually a common sense idea: most people learn to cope with adversity and, in so doing, develop inner strength, character, and wisdom. In short, post-traumatic growth is the process by which we change in positive ways after enduring a serious trauma.

It's important to note that some people who have unintentionally harmed recoil at the idea of post-traumatic growth. We've been told more than once, "I don't want to benefit from the worst thing I've ever done in my life."

We've also heard people who have experienced other kinds of trauma express appreciation for their hardship, such as, "I went through hell when I got cancer, but I'm a better person now" or "I didn't realize how much people cared until we lost our home in the tornado." Unintentional harm is not like that. We don't know anyone who would say, "I'm grateful because accidentally harming someone made me a better person."

All of us will forever regret what happened. We will never be "grateful" for the unintentional harm we have caused.

However, we can be grateful in our particular situation.

When we own who and where we are and create as much good as we can from these tragedies, we can experience gratitude.

After all, becoming another victim or endlessly punishing ourselves is not good for us, our families, our friends, or our communities. Why not resolve to emerge from trauma and moral injury with new strengths and insights? Why not accept the invitation that tragedy offers to reconsider our lives, our values, and our relationships?

Researchers say post-traumatic growth does not just happen. It takes self-reflection, focused attention, and effort. We believe it's a worthy goal.

We will share several ways people have experienced growth after a serious trauma. Depending on when your incident occurred and how you are coping, you might identify with one or more of these.

If your accident was recent and you are still in the grip of PTSD and moral injury, ask yourself which of these benefits appeals to you. Then, hold onto it as a goal. Giving yourself something positive to strive for can remind you that you are on a journey and that you can and will find your way out of whatever swamp or desert you may be in at present.

Possible Post-traumatic Growth Benefits

■ Confidence in our ability to rely on ourselves and to manage difficulties: "If I've survived this, I can handle anything."

■ Greater appreciation for life: "Now I understand that life is precious and fragile."

- Emotional expressiveness: "I am better able to talk about my feelings."

- Greater appreciation for others: "My family/friends stood by me in the darkest days. I am fortunate to have them in my life."

- Compassion: "I know what it feels like to be depressed, afraid, and despairing. I can relate, and I can offer support to others in need."

- Open-minded: "I'm less judgmental than I used to be. We all make mistakes."

- Clearer sense of priorities and values: "I've learned what's important in life."

- Spiritual development: "I feel a deeper sense of connection to God."

- Sense of meaning: "I want my life to mean something and I'm willing to work for that."

- Care for others: "I will do my best to keep my loved ones and my community safe."

- Kindness: "We all make mistakes. We all have weaknesses. I can respond with understanding and empathy. I try to help people when I can."

- Wisdom: "I make better decisions, I better understand myself and others, and I understand what I can and cannot control."

Source: *Posttraumatic Growth: Positive Changes in the Aftermath of Crisis* by R.G. Tedeschi, C.L. Park, and L.G. Calhoun.

Trauma can make us stronger, and it can also make us more vulnerable. In the realm of football or mixed martial arts, vulnerability is the opposite of strength. In the realm of emotions, however, vulnerability is a sign of strength. It takes strength to express and feel our feelings, to speak honestly, and to let others touch our hearts with their words and their caring. This gives us even more strength.

How do we foster post-traumatic growth? First, we hold the intention. We keep our goals in mind. Second, we talk with a therapist, clergy, or another trusted mentor. These conversations can help us see ourselves more clearly, clarify our values and beliefs, and plan accordingly. Third, we practice self-compassion. And fourth, we act.

What does that look like as we enter this new life, after unintentional harm? We believe it begins with our victim.

Legacy-Centered Growth

Part of the healing process is being able to talk frankly about what we've done and the people we've harmed, including ourselves. We are no longer avoiding and burying these things because the work we have done has, for the most part, removed the sting. Perhaps your PTSD symptoms are much better, your day-to-day life seems okay, and you can reflect back on your life. So, you can begin by taking steps to honor your victims and yourself and embark upon what we call Legacy-Centered Growth.

Of course, we can never "make up for" unintentionally killing someone. But we can resolve to honor the memory of our victims and all those who grieved and suffered—and that includes you. We can resolve to live virtuous lives, not because we are bad people who must live in shame, but because we have learned important lessons about the value and fragility of life. We can use our newfound strength and compassion to build community, put beauty into the world, and help others thrive through our love and support.

As we make and implement our plans, we further our own growth. We develop new skills, build new connections to others, and like ourselves better. We combat our tendencies to withdraw, isolate, ruminate, and hide from life. We even enjoy ourselves.

And isn't that, ultimately, a beautiful tribute to our victims? We have accepted accountability, struggled with our mental health, made positive changes in our lives, and now we are ready to affirm life, with full knowledge that tragedy can strike at any moment.

There are hundreds of ways we can honor our victims. Here are just a few ideas offered by some of our Fellowship members:

- Promoting safety by writing editorials, giving speeches, joining advocacy groups, writing to legislators, etc. Elizabeth worked with pedestrian and bicyclist advocacy groups to share her perspective while supporting their work.

- Creating beauty through music, visual arts, writing, filmmaking, etc. Such art does not need to be about the victim or the experience of unintentional harm, although it can be. Tony created a video about his car crash; Forrest puts short videos that offer hope and empathy for those in psychological pain on TikTok.

- Volunteering at a hospital, food kitchen, after-school program, senior center, animal shelter, etc. A number of Hyacinth Fellowship members volunteer as peer supporters, offering encouragement and mentoring to those who have more recently caused unintentional harm.

- Remembering your victim and their loved ones in daily prayers or intentions, etc. Jenn produces and hosts a Christian podcast in which she interviews a wide variety of people about how they have transcended trauma.

- Visiting an elderly or home-bound neighbor once a week. Robert checks on a disabled member of his community and helps with small tasks in her apartment.

- Raising money for a cause you or your victim cares about. Anita writes grants and solicits funding for the Hyacinth Fellowship.

- Spending more time with family or designating a special day of the month that you devote to your child—maybe you go to the beach or zoo, bake cookies, or play catch. Josie started hiking with her daughter soon after her incident, and one summer, they backpacked together for two weeks.

- Complete your education or seek training in a new field so that you can more fully develop your potential. Mark and Hugh are training to become therapists so they can help others cope with trauma, addiction, and depression.

- Reaching out to others who have unintentionally harmed. Brooke started a self-care book club specifically for those who have unintentionally harmed.

- Writing an article or book about your incident. David has written extensively about his experiences, which has not only helped him process his feelings and experiences but has also helped others who have unintentionally harmed.

- Advocating for those who have unintentionally harmed. Kim contacts first responders, giving talks and literature to those who make initial contact with those who unintentionally harm, instructing them on best practices and care guidelines.

- Writing a presentation for schools and community groups that can educate people about the subject of unintentional harm. Maryann delivered a sensational TED Talk and Debi regularly visits school assemblies.

Taking action should not feel like a punishment. It might feel like a challenge. You might even feel ambivalent about making a new commitment. But ultimately this is intended to expand and open your life in ways that feel good.

You might have to try a few times before settling on what feels right to you. Maryann volunteered in an adult literacy program, enrolled in a creative writing workshop, and tried to start a support group before deciding to create a website. Making the website used her intellectual skills and writing abilities without requiring risks that went too far beyond her comfort level. It turned out to be the right fit and now, more than 20 years later, the website has reached thousands of people worldwide.

Key Takeaways

* Most people who are accidental killers will recover and heal from the trauma. It may take months or years, but eventually—and often with therapy and deliberate practices—you will find healing and wholeness. There is no timeline for this journey, and there will likely be relapses caused by triggers that plunge you back into distress. Knowing the triggers and developing healthy coping mechanisms can help. It's also important to acknowledge that you can experience post-traumatic growth, ways in which you have learned about your strength and resilience, grown in compassion, more engaged in doing your part to make this world a better, kinder, safer place.

Discussion Questions

1. Do you see a light at the end of the tunnel? Do you think it's possible to regain your emotional footing and find a place of peace and healing after the accident? What steps can you take toward that goal?

2. Identify some situations that have been or could be triggers for you. What are some coping methods that you can practice and help you to manage those triggers?

3. Is the event anniversary difficult for you? What are some ways that you might honor your victim on this day?

4. Do you think you've experienced some post-traumatic growth? If it's difficult for you to articulate any areas of growth, ask a spouse, partner, or friend. They might be able to see ways that you've grown and developed.

5. How can you put your skills, beliefs, and interests toward honoring your victims? How can you honor your own journey?

Afterword

I'm not sure which feeling is greater: my deep fondness and appreciation for the life and work of a great human being, Maryann Gray, or my deep and profound sadness in having to write these words without her.

My dear co-author, co-laborer, and friend died suddenly and unexpectedly in April 2023 during the writing of this book.

In the fledgling field of our pursuit, helping those who unintentionally harm others, Maryann Gray is a legend. She pioneered acceptance, understanding, and compassion as she reminded thousands of people that it hurts to hurt others. She sought out, inspired, and initiated science-based research while grounding her work in loving, personal relationships with people whom she affectionately called CADIs (Causing Accidental Death or Injury) believing hers to be, at its heart, a deeply spiritual enterprise.

Maryann's work was rooted in suffering.

Her experience in graduate school of winding through the back roads of Southern Ohio on a clear, summery morning when 8-year-old Brian darted in front of her car, shaped nearly every day that followed.

He died, as did a part of her.

Consequently, a seed fell to the ground and, like a hyacinth, grew into something of great beauty and fragrance that has made life better for so many who have done what she did.

Maryann put her pain to purpose when, in 2003, she founded a website that she called "Accidental Impacts." She filled it with practical resources for people who cause unintentional harm. Today, the site—and umbrella organization—has grown exponentially and is known as the Hyacinth Fellowship. In doing this work, Maryann gave voice and validity to a massive tribe of people who live in the shadows of shame and guilt brought on by the unintentional harm they have caused.

Maryann was one of the most profound embodiments of compassion I've ever known: selfless, generous, and gifted with more intelligence than the vast majority of us. I am ever grateful she chose to use those gifts for the betterment of humanity.

This book is our offering of hope and companionship for everyone who has unintentionally harmed. The tragedies that beset us do topple, grieve, and haunt us. But they also have the potential to make us more compassionate, caring, and understanding of the breadth of our human condition.

You are not your worst mistake.

You can recover from this.

You can, like a hyacinth, grow into something more beautiful than you think.

I stand in humble gratitude alongside a mourning multitude of Maryann's CADIs, all determined to put our pain to purpose by carrying on this work, her work, to the generations that follow. I invite you to support the Hyacinth Fellowship with your time, talent, or treasure by visiting our website and making a donation. Together we can help, heal, and build a more compassionate world.

—Chris Yaw

All proceeds from this book go to The Hyacinth Fellowship, a 501c3 nonprofit charity.

About the Authors

Maryann Jacobi Gray

As the founder and driving force behind The Hyacinth Fellowship, Maryann Jacobi Gray worked as a social psychologist and educator and most recently served as assistant provost at UCLA. She also worked at RAND, a research and analysis organization, as a behavioral science researcher and at the University of Southern California as an associate vice provost.

When Maryann was 22 years old, she unintentionally killed an 8-year-old boy who darted in front of her car. She spoke and wrote widely about the challenges facing those who unintentionally harm or kill others for more than 20 years.

Chris Yaw

Chris is an Episcopal priest and pastors a church in Metro Detroit. He holds two graduate degrees in theology and has advocated for the homeless, hungry, and those harmed by gun violence.

His life was forever changed after his friend and gardener was crushed to death in a garage door that Chris had cut corners to install. As president of The Hyacinth Fellowship, Chris has helped guide the organization in the turbulent years following Maryann's death.

Made in the USA
Columbia, SC
25 September 2024